MW00640581

TURNING THE HEARTS OF FATHERS

Milk and Cookies Will Change the World

MARK SANDFORD

Armour

Turning the Hearts of Fathers:
Milk and Cookies Will Change the World

© Mark Sandford 2022

Published by Armour Books
P. O. Box 492, Corinda, QLD 4075 AUSTRALIA

Cover Images:
Kevin Carden / Lightstock | Description: Father and Daughter in the Rain.
konradlew / istockphoto | Description: Winding Farm Road through Foggy Landscape -
fields, meadow, sun during sunrise

Cookies & milk icon: Dimensions Design (edited)

Cover & Interior Design and Typeset by Beckon Creative

ISBN: 978-1-925380-439

A catalogue record for this
book is available from the
National Library of Australia

All rights reserved. No part of this publication may be reproduced, stored in, or introduced
into a retrieval system, or transmitted, in any form, or by any means (electronic,
mechanical, photocopying, recording or otherwise) without the prior written permission of
the publisher.

Unless otherwise indicated, Scripture quotations are taken from the New American Standard Bible®,
Copyright © 1960, 1962, 1963, 1968, 1971, 1972, 1973, 1975, 1977, 1995 by The Lockman
Foundation. Used by permission. (www.Lockman.org)

Scripture quotations marked NIV are taken from the Holy Bible, New International Version®, NIV®.
Copyright © 1973, 1978, 1984, 2011 by Biblica, Inc.™ Used by permission of Zondervan. All rights
reserved worldwide. www.zondervan.com The "NIV" and "New International Version" are trademarks
registered in the United States Patent and Trademark Office by Biblica, Inc.™

Scripture quotations marked NKJV are taken from the New King James Version. Copyright © 1982 by
Thomas Nelson, Inc. Used by permission. All rights reserved.

TURNING THE HEARTS OF FATHERS

Milk and Cookies Will Change the World

MARK SANDFORD

I dedicate this book to:

My parents, John and Paula Sandford, who planted in my heart and the hearts of thousands the urgency of Elijah's call to "turn the hearts of the fathers to their children."

Maureen, my partner in learning to answer that call.

Our three children, Míchal, Jonah, and Jasha, from whom we are now learning as much about Elijah's call as we taught them when they were little.

My brother, Loren, who is now at home with Elijah and in the arms of the Father. During the last four years of his earthly life, he was a spiritual father to Maureen and me at a time when we most needed one.

Miss Angela Branz, my twelfth-grade creative writing teacher. During a dark season when my confidence was low, she made me believe I could be a good writer.

… And of course, the prophet Elijah, whose calling in Malachi 4:5-6 "to turn the hearts of the fathers to their children and the hearts of the children to their fathers" is the inspiration for this book.

CONTENTS

CHAPTER 1

The Miracle of Milk and Cookies

LATE ONE NIGHT IN 1958, my father, John Sandford, woke up praying in a language he had never spoken or even heard of. (This was two years before the Charismatic Movement began!) As a pastor in a Protestant denomination that had long forgotten the supernatural moves of God, he was so unfamiliar with spiritual gifts that he didn't even know what this was. He passed it by a few fellow pastors; some of them must have wondered if he was losing his grip on reality! Fortunately, an elderly Pentecostal preacher was able to fill him in on what was happening. He was praying in tongues, a gift bestowed on the church at Pentecost (Acts 2:4).

And so it was that from the age of three I grew up in a household where the supernatural was counted on as surely as the morning sun. As I look back over the years, I can't imagine what we would have done without the Holy Spirit's interventions; at times, our very lives depended on them. How safe it felt to know we could rely on Dad's spiritual gifts to keep away danger! He was awakened one night at 2:00 am, sensing a call to pray that my older my brother Loren (on an overnight trip with his rock band) would be spared from death in a car accident. At the very moment when Dad prayed, Loren was startled awake—behind the wheel, going seventy miles per hour! He heard a voice calling his name, and he slammed on the brake just in time to keep from jamming our family's car under the back of a semi!

Dad started a trend in our family that has repeatedly saved the lives of my own children. Like the night on a ministry trip to Chicago when Maureen whispered, "Mark, wake up! You need to pray for Míchal [the oldest of our three children] or she'll die in an accident!" We prayed, then dialed her up.

No response. We called again.

"Hello?" Her voice sounded groggy. She was on her way home from a late-night gospel concert on the Columbia River gorge near George, Washington (yes, there really is such a town) and had fallen fast asleep going seventy miles per hour down Interstate 90! Many times throughout the years, members of our family would have been killed or injured if God had not warned one of us and we had not prayed. Every time, we were sobered by the fact that, once again, my parents' example had saved our lives. God's warnings never frightened us. Mom and Dad had taught us not to fear; we knew that God would always be there when we called.

When I was fourteen, that took the edge off my apprehension about a painful surgery. Nineteen plantar warts had grown deep into the bottom of my foot. In those days (the late 1960's), the doctor had to literally dig them out with a scalpel, and a shot of anesthetic wouldn't kill all the pain. Although I can't say I wasn't afraid, I managed to sleep well enough the night before the operation. After all, if Mom and Dad prayed, how bad could it be? The next morning, my foot was completely healed, and much to my relief, surgery was cancelled!

We always knew that life would go just as God had planned, because Mom and Dad always knew He had a plan. Dad saw Maureen in a dream fourteen years before I met her and felt prompted to pray that my heart would be open when the time came for our paths to cross. A few years after we married, after ministering for a season in Leesburg,

Florida, Maureen and I were asked to join the pastoral staff at a church in Jupiter, Florida (yes, there really is a town named that, too).

Then Dad called. "Normally, I would think it's wrong to tell you what steps to take in your career. But God is telling me that moving to Jupiter is a trap. It's time to come home to Idaho." We prayed and felt the Holy Spirit confirm this. Three weeks after we arrived in Idaho, the church in Jupiter split, and more than half of the church left. There wouldn't have been enough remaining parishioners to provide us with a living wage! We watched that ship sink from our safe vantage point nearly three thousand miles away, grateful that my father's prophetic warning had gathered us into the shelter of God's favor.

We also learned that if we deliberately and continually opposed God's will, we could forfeit such favor. As children, my brothers and sisters and I watched Dad warn the local churches to get on their knees on behalf of Wallace, Idaho, the little mountain community where we lived at the time. In the early 1970's, it was rife with prostitution, illegal gambling, and a multitude of other sins (there were five brothels in a town of two thousand, two hundred!). He prophesied about the Sunshine Mine disaster but promised that if the churches would repent on behalf of the community, it would be prevented. They didn't, and it wasn't. Ninety-one miners died.

And we learned that God allows some things to happen for reasons only He knows. Dad dreamed about the assassination of President Kennedy and the resignation of President Nixon. My parents prayed (I suspect that many across the nation were also called to pray). The Holy Spirit intervened by exposing the corruption in the Nixon administration. But why did he allow President Kennedy to die? We never found out. We learned to trust God with unanswered questions. For so many others in the decades after World War 2, church was a pretentious display of religious airs, but Mom and Dad made God real. But what made Him seem most real was neither the prophecies nor the miracles. It was how these supernatural blessings came to us—through the very "warf and woop" of life, as Dad phrased it. Heaven came calling amid family picnics and board games around the dining room table as we dunked graham crackers in milk. Mom filled our kitchen with the scent of heaven—it smelled like fresh-baked cornbread smothered with butter beans and molasses, pumpkin pie, and no-bake chocolate cookies firming up on sheets of wax paper. Around our big oak dinner table, between bites, Dad expounded upon his latest revelations. I have come to understand that in moments like these, the supernatural wasn't a stranger intruding into our otherwise ordinary earthly life. God was the very life from which sprang both the miracles of prophecy and healing and the miracle of milk and cookies.

I must confess that for a season our family was tempted to make signs and wonders an end in and of themselves—to the point of making idols of them. I can't say that those gifts have lost their sparkle. But I can say their sparkle isn't the distraction it once was. The Cross has a way of polishing a better shine on the simpler things of life. A heart that learns to love is a heart that learns to see just as much sparkle in milk and cookies as in the supernatural, if not more so.

After a lifetime of answering the call to take up our cross and follow Jesus, my brothers and sisters and I look back on the little revival around our kitchen table and view its sparkle from God's perspective. It was all a miracle. And it was all ordinary. And it was all just the way life was supposed to be.

CHAPTER 2

Where's That Revival God Promised?

WHEN I WAS A CHILD, for many believers, church didn't hold out much sparkle. Attendance at a bland weekly ritual was the price paid to give God His due and keep up appearances. Then came the Charismatic Renewal. Suddenly, Jesus was alive! He walked and talked with us. He worked miracles. The words of the Lord's prayer, *"Thy kingdom come, Thy will be done, on earth as it is in heaven,"* were made real! So, when fellow Christians discovered the spiritual gifts that my family had already known for some time, I was puzzled at my own response.

"It's coming soon! I know it!" Gary* could hardly catch his breath. "It's gonna be the greatest revival the world has ever seen! It'll transform our nation! I feel it might happen in the next few months. I'm absolutely sure it'll happen in the next few years!"

Gary looked to me for a rousing confirmation. I wanted to believe him. I wanted revival as much as anyone. Everyone was talking about it. But I couldn't sense it coming any time soon. "What's wrong with me?" I thought. I tried to work up a little enthusiasm. "Yeah, that'll be good ... if it happens."

Gary cocked his head, scrutinized me through the corner of his eye, and playfully feigned a disapproving frown. "Whadaya mean, *if* it happens?" He threw his arm around my shoulder and chided me with

---

* "Gary" is a composite of several persons.

a chuckle, "What's the matter with you? Have a little faith!" And he earnestly promised, "Hey, don't worry! Just wait and see. It'll happen!"

… It didn't happen.

I'm not talking about the next year. Or even the next decade. The year was 1973; I was eighteen and in my first year of college. The renewal was just coming out of its infancy. "Signs and wonders" were on everyone's tongue. Mystical gifts were embraced as a staple of everyday life. Renewal had caught fire among Catholics as well. Surely revival was just around the corner!

When revival didn't materialize, oddly, no one seemed fazed. Believers shrugged it off and raised their hopes again. And again, it didn't happen. And again. And again. Every few years there were more "prophecies" that revival was on our doorstep. Excitement mounted to a fever pitch … and then evaporated into thin air. No one seemed to recall the last ten times we had received this amazing "new" prophetic revelation. As feverish anticipation repeatedly cycled past, I began to feel like I was living in a sci-fi movie; aliens kept slipping an amnesia-inducing drug into the water supply.

From time to time, movements did pop up to make a significant difference, such as the Jesus People and the "Toronto Blessing." But not the big one. Not the next "Great Awakening" that was expected to set the world ablaze and powerfully impact our culture.

After a lifetime of watching tsunamis of joyous expectation wash by, I have come to realize my eighteen-year-old heart didn't lack faith at all. What it did lack was confidence in what my spirit was accurately sensing. Yes, God wanted to send a great revival. But we weren't ready; something was missing.

In the forty-eight years since my conversation with Gary, I have asked the Holy Spirit many times, "Where's that promised revival? Why is it so long in coming?" The Western world, like an unanchored ship, drifts aimlessly into the gathering storm. Even some of God's people are pulling up anchor and drifting along with it.

And yet, God tarries …

At a Christian leaders' conference, the latest "new" revelation of imminent revival was racing through the gathering like wildfire through a munitions factory. In a quaint little coffee shop nearby, happy proclamations bubbled up through the din like popcorn: "It's coming soon!" "Maybe in the next few months!" "Surely in the coming year!" While savoring a draft of mint tea, I took a quick mental scan of the last half-century and mused, "Am I experiencing déjà vu?"

I seemed to sense the Holy Spirit telling me why a revival was, in fact, not imminent. "Am I hearing you correctly?" I prayed. The answer came quickly. A leader who personally knew most of those in attendance was asked, "How many here would you say are neglecting their children for the sake of the ministry?"

"I'd guess about four out of five."

I wondered if that estimate was too kind. I could count on one hand with fingers to spare, fellow preachers' kids whose dads didn't fit that description. Later, an informal poll revealed that nearly half the audience had prodigal children who were walking away from God.

I felt a nudge from the Holy Spirit to step up to the mic and share some thoughts about these trends. "There's a lot of excitement here about a coming revival. I believe God wants that for us!" I let that happy thought sink in for a moment. "But there's a reason why He hasn't sent it yet. I know this might sound strange, but I sense that so far, God has *protected* us from revival." That statement furrowed a few brows. "The reason being that if God had given us a revival before now, it might have actually harmed our nation." More eyebrows were raised.

I read Malachi 4:5–6 (NKJV) to them: *"Behold, I will send you Elijah the prophet before the coming of the great and dreadful day of the*

Lord. And He will turn the hearts of the fathers to their children, and the hearts of the children to their fathers, lest I come and smite the earth with a curse."

Then I connected the dots. "If revival comes, we leaders will have a lot more ministry to do, and we'll neglect our children even more than we do now. They'll resent us for it, and they'll have even more reason to walk away from God. This may bring the curse of Malachi 4:5–6 upon us, and the revival that was meant to transform our nation may actually harm it." Before hearts could begin to sink, I reassured them, "I believe God wants revival for us. All we have to do is repent to God and our children and make them our priority. If we do, we'll be more ready for revival, and it may come quickly. I sense that God is giving us a gift of extra time to respond to Elijah's call *before* revival finally hits, so that our children will be more likely to follow."

This was a gift few had been hoping for.

I didn't see much fire in their eyes about what I was sharing, and as the next speaker took the stage, I could sense the embers fading. By the end of the day, the conference was alive again with perky declarations: "It's coming soon!" "In the next few months!" "Certainly, within the next year!"

That was many years ago.

Throughout the decades, occasionally I've heard isolated voices calling us back to the bottom line. *"Signs and wonders,"* they say, *"will follow those who believe'* [Mark 16:17], not the other way around! Repentance precedes any revival."

"Oh yes, repentance; we need to remember that." That is always the somber reply. And for the moment, people really mean it. But the moment always passes. Happy banter about signs and wonders and the next revival rushes back in as predictably as the returning tide. Thoughts of repentance silently wash back out into the vast nowhere, and with it, thoughts of repenting to our children.

I don't mean to disparage the gifts. Having grown up in the Sandford family, how can I? And how can I be untrue to the promises of Christ? *"The one who believes in Me, the works that I do, he will do also; and greater works than these he will do"* (John 14:12). Should we not stand in joyful expectation of this? St. Paul urged us to eagerly desire the higher gifts (1 Corinthians 14:1). May they be ours in abundance in a revival that that will change the world!

But not yet. Not until our hearts learn to yearn for what comes first—the milk and cookies that give miracles their fuller context, and thus, their true meaning.

In the early days of the Charismatic Movement, we were babes enthralled with the tinsel and multicolored lights, our eyes aglow with the supernatural goodies we were unwrapping. There was nothing reprehensible about our immaturity; every movement must have its infancy. But there was so much more under the tree to discover.

Over the decades, the unwrapping has continued until the makings of a revival are mostly in place. Worship is no longer the dry ritual of my childhood; for many, it has become a transcendent visit to the throne room. Evangelism is no longer just for missionaries in the jungles of Borneo. It's what you do on the streets and in the coffee shops and at the water cooler. Intercessory prayer groups have sprung up in every city and town, pleading with God for the hearts of the nation.

… But where is there equal passion for the key that will enable us to pass on these blessings to the next generation? Worship, evangelism, and prophetic intercessory prayer can transport us to the highest halls of spiritual pleasure, and well they should. Repentance is not nearly as much fun. But unless it becomes our foremost concern, none of these spiritual blessings will incite a world-changing revival. And even if they do, if we repent to God but not also to the next generation, who will keep the fervor going when we are gone?

You know you've grown up when you take more pleasure in giving gifts to your children than in unwrapping your own presents. As a parent, you wrap God's sacrificial love in the most ordinary packages—hugs and kisses even when you're not feeling particularly affectionate, playtime and tickles when you'd rather be watching the evening news, laying aside your favorite novel to read bedtime stories. This may not be as exciting as the fireworks at a revival, but it will have much more staying power. And it's what will make the effects of revival last beyond our generation.

In the end, it is milk and cookies that will change the world. It takes a lot of growing pains for a heart to grasp that simple truth. How little did we know just how long and trying that process could be …

CHAPTER 3

Why is God Putting Me Through This?

My old friend Gary* had had as much he could take with the growing pains. "Why is God putting me through this?" He sucked in a deep breath, pursed his lips, puffed out his cheeks, and heaved an exasperated sigh. "I've been serving God for … how long?" He surveyed the air as if scanning an imaginary spread sheet. "Thirty years! Thirty years ago, a famous prophetic leader told me I had an important task ahead of me—I would reach thousands for the gospel."

The forty-plus years since our discussion about revival had tempered Gary's youthful zeal, but not his determined faith. "I know I have a gift for that. There've been times when I sat down next to someone on a bus and, by the time we got to the next stop, he'd given his life to Christ! I don't mean to complain, because it's so wonderful when that happens. I'm grateful, and I'll keep on doing it till the day I die. But, a few weeks after I was promised this bright future, it felt like God went away and left me on a deserted island. I couldn't feel His presence anymore. I couldn't hear Him. I asked Him where He'd gone. He never answered."

"Gary, have you heard of the 'dark night of the soul'"?

"No; what's that?" he asked, although I could tell he intuitively identified with the phrase. I sensed that the feel of what I was about

---

* "Gary" is a composite of several persons.

to share would not be unfamiliar to him. I explained that the man who wrote the book, *Dark Night of the Soul*, in 1568, a Catholic saint known as John of the Cross, felt cut off from God for a season, much like Gary. John's dear friend Teresa of Avila had asked him to help her reform the nuns in the Carmelite order over whom she had charge. John steered them back toward their vow of poverty and a disciplined life of prayer.[1] His and Teresa's prayer-life brought them so close to the heart of God that they were seen floating together off the ground in rapturous adoration!

Such fervor was lost on monks who despised St. John's reforms. They actually kidnapped him and took him to trial before a court of friars. He was charged with "disobedience," even though his actions had been endorsed by the Pope! They shoved him into a cramped cell dimly lit through high, narrow windows, where he bore up under the chill of winter and the stifling heat of summer. His clothes were never washed and became lice-infested.[2] They allowed him a meager meal of bread and water only three times a week—and only if he agreed to submit to a public lashing every time![3] After nine months, weak and emaciated, somehow, he managed to loosen the screws on the lock, lift the door off its hinges, and escape. If he had waited just a few more weeks, he might have perished.

While St. John was still in prison, a kind monk who had been appointed as his jailer smuggled paper, pen, and ink to him. By meager candlelight, he wrote about his dark night, which felt darker to him than his dismal prison cell.[4]

Before my conversation with Gary, Maureen and I had counseled so many who had been through a similar experience. At the very time when they most needed to hear the Holy Spirit's reassuring voice, they could neither hear him nor feel His presence. Life fell flat and seemed to lose meaning. No joy. No excitement. Many lost favor with others who were no longer drawn to their ministry or their gifts. They were mocked and mistreated. Many endured powerful temptations. Although they succeeded in resisting, it still felt like God wasn't there to help. Although they knew better, they felt as if God had abandoned them.

Gary resonated with these struggles. But with a hint of skepticism, he asked, "Is the 'dark night of the soul' mentioned in Scripture?"

"Not by that name," I answered, "but St. John never called it that. Others came up with that phrase. He just called it the 'dark night,'[5] and Scripture does talk about God taking us through dark times. Jeremiah went through a kind of dark night, similar to John's in a lot of ways."

I opened my Bible and turned to Chapter 3 of Lamentations. "In verse two, Jeremiah says, *'He has driven me away and made me walk in* **darkness** *rather than light.'* In verse three, he says, *'He has turned His hand against me again and again, all day long.'* In the dark night, it feels that way. Although as a prophet, Jeremiah didn't stop hearing God, he didn't feel like God was hearing *him*; in verse eight, he says, *'Even when I cry out or call for help, He shuts out my prayer.'* During the dark night, you can lose favor with people; in verse fourteen Jeremiah says, *'I became the laughingstock of all my people; they mock me in song all day long'"* (Lamentations 3:2; 3; 8; 14 NIV).

"I totally see what you're saying, but surely God doesn't wanna make us miserable for no reason. What's the point of all of this?"

So many others had asked me that question. In more than three decades as a prayer counselor, I had never seen so many going through such struggles as I had in the last several years. "When you're going through it," I answered, "it can feel like it's all for nothing. But I think that's because a lot of people think the dark night is a time when God withdraws His presence from you. St. John believed that surprisingly, it's not. It's actually a time when He increases it!"[6]

Gary cocked his head and leaned a little closer.

"I agree that God doesn't withdraw His presence; nowhere does Scripture say that God withdraws from people who are true to Him. It says, 'He'll never leave you nor forsake you.' St. John took it a step further; he said God increases His presence so much that your spirit gets overloaded. You might say it's like when lightning strikes near your house, and there's a power surge, and all the lights go out. As an immature Christian, you can get so excited about the things of God—the high you feel in His presence, the mystical experiences, the fireworks. To keep you from loving these things more than God, He draws so close to you that you 'short circuit' for a while. I suspect that at least in some cases, St. John may be right about that. And maybe sometimes it's just the pain that makes you go numb. In any case, God doesn't withdraw His presence, but it still feels like He has put you on what St. John called a 'spiritual diet.'[7] At first, life can feel empty. But a time comes when the spiritual numbness wears off and you start to feel again. It's a quieter, sweeter communion with God. And it's so much more satisfying than the excitement you felt before. In verse twenty-four, Jeremiah says, *The Lord is my portion. … Therefore, I wait for Him.'* Jeremiah got to the point where he felt he had nothing left—not the highs, not the fireworks, not the favor of other people. He had only one portion left—the Lord Himself. That's *all* he had. But there comes a time when that's all you care about. It's not that you don't want those other experiences anymore. It's more like you just don't need them. You just need Jesus. You feel satisfied with just Him. And for that reason, He can trust you with supernatural experiences more than ever before, because He knows you won't make idols out of them."

Gary's eyes brightened; a heavy load was lifting.

"Over and over in the Bible, when God called someone to an important task, He put them through a season of trial to prepare them for it. It didn't always look like St. John's dark night. It didn't always mean they couldn't hear God or feel His presence. But it was always some kind of suffering, people were often left in the dark about why God allowed it. Like Moses' forty years as a shepherd after holding a high position in Pharaoh's household. Until he saw the burning bush on Mt. Sinai, there was no promise he'd ever be anything but a shepherd. Or Joseph being sold into slavery and then put in prison for a crime he didn't commit. He couldn't know how he'd ever get out and live out the dreams God had given him. Or—"

"—Or David being chased by Saul's armies for years, when he didn't deserve it," Gary said. "I've been through a dark night. I just didn't know what to call it."

"There's been an increase of people going through it," I continued. "It seems like so many are from our generation. I've had a sense that as we come out of our dark night, we'll need to be on the alert to mentor younger Christians through their own struggles and help bring them into a lighter place. Many of them have never known what it's like to have a father or mother walk through trials with them."

Gary nodded thoughtfully. "That helps. Just knowing I'm not the only one. It means God must have some kind of master plan that makes this all worthwhile."

I had wondered, how many other Garys are out there? In recent years, I had asked audiences in the US, Canada, East Asia, Europe, and Australia, "How many of you have been going through a dark night of the soul?" Every time, many hands had shot up. Was I witnessing a trend? Fellow believers assured me that they, too, had seen a trend. "We thought the Holy Spirit had promised that a great move of God is coming. It's been prophesied so many times! Instead, we get this. Why is God putting us through this?"

Aside from the need to help younger strugglers, I could see an answer in Gary's circumstances: there was no more effective way to cultivate a lifestyle of repentance and a balanced view of the Christian life. Many Christians, especially Protestants, have thought the born-again experience nearly instantly transforms character. But, in earlier centuries, Christians always understood that character is built through a lifelong process. Orthodox Christians call this process "theosis" (from the Greek word, *Theos*, meaning "God")—continual repentance and devotion that brings us into ever-increasing intimacy with God and transforms us into His likeness. As St. Paul said: *"We all, with unveiled faces, looking as in a mirror at the glory of the Lord, are being transformed into the same image **from glory to glory**"* (2 Corinthians 3:18, emphasis mine).

In the early 300's AD, Saint Athanasias coined the phrase that became the tagline for theosis: "The Son of God became man so that we might become God."[8] Of course he didn't mean we literally become God. But the transformation of hearts so thrilled him that he could describe it only through hyperbole (pronounced, hie-pér-bo-lee), a figure of speech common at the time—an over-the-top exaggeration to emphasize a point. A modern example: "She was an absolute angel"). Athanasius simply meant what St. Paul meant when he said, *"It is no longer I who live, but Christ lives in me"* (Galatians 2:20).

In an instant, Gary had chosen to receive Christ into his heart, but he was learning that the transformation of his character would take much longer. Nothing drives home that truth more than the dark night. During that season, there are few spiritual ecstasies in which to take refuge. You can no longer use your impressive spiritual gifts to deceive yourself into overestimating how Christlike you have become. Until the highs return, you must turn your heart to God for help again and again, even when you feel like He's not there.

In a warm fatherly tone, I assured Gary, "You know, Gary, the reason you're in the dark night isn't because you've done anything wrong. God isn't displeased with you. And you're not reaping any evil you've sown. I know this might sound really strange, but the dark night is a way God is actually *rewarding* you."

With a note of dry humor, Gary retorted, "Oh really? Why doesn't He reward someone else?!!" We both laughed, but I knew that on some level he was dead serious.

"Yeah," I replied, "I know it feels that way. But God is pleased with you because He knows He can trust you. He knows you have the maturity to not give up. He's putting you through this because He knows it'll build into you the kind of character that'll make you ready for whatever's on the other side of this trial. There'll come a time when you get so close to the heart of Jesus that you'll see it really has been worth all the pain."

There had been a time when Gary was seduced by the modern delusion that spiritual maturity is not only instantly, but painlessly achieved. Now he was learning what, from the earliest days of the faith, God's people had always understood. In the early 400's AD, Augustine said, "God, by making us wait, stretches desire. Stretching desire, he stretches the soul. Stretching the soul, he makes it capable of receiving." And in the late 500's, St. Gregory the Great said: "The bride is hampered in her search so that this delay may increase the capacity for God, and that she may find one day more fully what she is seeking." In His kindness, God was leading Gary past the desert to where he could say, *"He makes me lie down in green pastures"* (Psalm 23:2 NIV).

I continued, "Maureen and I are starting to see how much it's been worth it, despite everything we've been through. Jesus really has become our portion. The excitement you've felt about signs and wonders will pale compared to the sweetness of just knowing Jesus on a deeper level than ever before. You'll begin to feel a softer, sweeter presence of God. It's so much better and long-lasting than the fireworks that come and go. It's a quieter yet stronger presence that's always there. You fall in love with Jesus like a baby falls in love with its Mom. You learn to rest in Him. It's so satisfying that you really do come to feel that the dark night was worth it. And what makes it even more worth it is that when you get so close to God that He becomes your portion, you want to pass that love on to the next generation."

For the moment, the part about the next generation didn't seem to register with Gary. He was focused on his own struggles. "Actually, I started to feel that sweet presence a couple of years ago," Gary said wistfully. "But as soon as things started getting better, all hell broke loose!" He sat back, clasped his fingers behind his head, took a deep breath, and yawned out his words: "It takes energy just to share everything that's happened." He paused to gather his thoughts. "After I received that prophecy about reaching thousands for the gospel, I thought everything was gonna be so great. Other people gave me that same prophetic word. I had dreams at night about it too!" He flipped his hands up and shrugged. "I dunno. Did God really say all that, or didn't He?"

Gary leaned forward and began to recount trials of the last two years—his job lost to a coworker who lied about him and flattered the boss. His wife's affair with his best friend. His agonizing struggle to woo her back and forgive them both. His opportunity to head up his church's worship team—just in time to see his pastor fired for embezzling church funds! The collapse of the church. The collapse of Gary's health.

I thought of the lists of woes others had shared with Maureen and me. As a prayer counselor and conference speaker, I'd been around the block enough times to see a pattern forming. Over the years, the number of people going through such trials had seemed to increase. I thought of Job in the Bible who complained about God, using the same word St. John of the Cross had used: *"He has shrouded my paths* *in **darkness***" (Job 19:8 NIV, emphasis mine). Job lost everything—his livelihood, his reputation, his children, and his health.

In the 1980's, when I began my work as a prayer counselor, most Christians I counseled suffered from specific struggles while leading otherwise satisfying lives. Now, to one degree or another, many of them felt like Job; for a season it had felt like suffering was their life. Many, coming out of the dark night, told us the same story: "I've jumped from the frying pan into the fire!" Just as they had begun once again to enjoy God's sweet presence, tragedy struck. Jobs were lost. Reputations were smeared. Friends betrayed them. Finances plummeted. Accidents and injuries befell them. Loved ones died unexpectedly; a few even lost a child. Blessedly, the losses most had suffered were not as extensive as those of Job. But, for a few, they had been.

"Is life really getting harder for many of your people?" I prayed. "Or am I just noticing the struggles more than I used to?" I filed back through my own recent past. The losses. The betrayals …

"Mark, are you alright?"

"Yeah, I'm alright. I was just thinking about struggles I've been through myself. And all the people I've counseled who've been through what you and I have been through."

"So you know what it feels like," said Gary. "I know I should feel grateful. But after all the no-wins, there's not much energy left to feel *anything*. Sometimes I've said, 'Lord, why don't You just take me home?' But I get up and face the day, not knowing where it's heading. Not knowing anything except that God is God, and that He must have some kind of plan in all of this." Gary let out a heavy sigh. "There are times when I've gotten so exasperated, I cussed out God. You wouldn't believe what came outta my mouth! There were times when I shook my fist and shouted, 'Leave me alone!' And then, of course, I begged His forgiveness. And then I got angry at Him again. And just when I felt like I couldn't take anymore, it got worse! There've been times when I've told God I would *never* treat my kids the way He treats His!"

Gary threw up his hands and asked again, "Whyyyyy is God putting me through this?!"

My answers thus far hadn't yet hit the "sweet spot" and calmed his uncertainty. I paused to consider his question and shrugged. "In the face of the pain you're feeling, how can any words I say suffice?" Something in Gary's expression told me he was granting me the grace to speak anyway. "All I know is what I've learned through my own losses. For a long time, every time I suffered a loss, I felt disillusioned with God. But I had to turn back to Him because ... well, who else was there to go to? Sometimes I didn't even know *how* to turn back to Him," I said with a little gallows laugh. "I had to *ask* Him how. Every time someone hurt me, I had to forgive. And it happened so many times that I learned that I really *couldn't* forgive. I had to ask God to do it through me. You get to the point where you don't even have the energy to turn back to God unless He helps you. It has to be a gift. We think of God giving gifts like tongues and healing and prophecy, but I've learned that *everything* is a gift. Even repentance!"

Gary nodded. "Yeah," he uttered in a voice I could barely hear. He was looking down, deep in thought yet still focused on what I was saying.

"And somewhere deep inside," I continued, "you give up. And it's a good kind of giving up. Because this rest—this really deep rest—comes over you. Maureen and are starting to feel that, and we feel a kind of joy we've never felt before. It's not the giddy kind of joy I felt when I first asked Jesus into my heart when I was eleven. It's quieter but more powerful. The closer I get to God, the more I can feel joy even when things don't feel like they're going right. The only way to get there is through learning on a deep, deep level what repentance really is. It's not just turning away from sin. It's turning your heart toward God until He is *everything* to you. I've had to turn to Him over and over to make it through. And in the process, I've started turning my heart to my kids more than ever, because I'm more focused on God than on myself. I'm convinced that much of what I've been through is for their sake—to get me to where my heart is focused on them, not me."

Gary looked up and nodded knowingly.

"I've always tried to turn toward my kids," I continued. "To be there for them. But my heart never knew how to keep that going." I paused a moment as I realized at a deeper level how empty that must have made them feel. "Not until my struggles made me turn to God again and again did I learn how to rely on Him as much as I do now. … Yeah," I said, as if hearing my own thoughts for the first time. "Sometimes you don't quite realize what you've been learning until you hear yourself say it out loud."

… And we both sat a while and let that thought sink in.

1   St. John of the Cross, E. Allison Peers, translator, *Dark Night of the Soul* (Mineola, NY: Dover Publications Inc., 2003), v.
2   "St. John of the Cross—Conflicts of Jurisdiction," *ICS Publications, Institute of Carmelite Studies*, Accessed Feb 3, 2021, https://www.icspublications.org/pages/saint-john-of-the-cross-conflicts-of-jurisdiction.
3   St. John of the Cross, Dark Night, v.
4   "St. John of the Cross," *Catholic Online*, Accessed Feb 2, 2021, https://www.catholic.org/saints/saint.php?saint_id=65.
5   Lawrence Cunningham, "Who was St. John of the Cross?", *America the Jesuit Review* (Jan. 30, 2006), Accessed Feb. 2, 2021, https://www.americamagazine.org/faith/2006/01/30/who-was-st-john-cross.
6   St. John of the Cross, *Dark Night*, 47–48.
7   St. John of the Cross, *Dark Night*, 84.
8   St. Athanasius, *On the Incarnation*, 54:3.

CHAPTER 4

Finding the Next Generation

IN 2008, ONE OF THE PURPOSES for what Gary and I and so many others had been going through was beginning to unfold. While I was traveling and teaching in Australia, a man at a seminar told me to keep an eye out for a man who was searching for a deeper relationship with God. "God will give you an encouraging word for him," he said.

I called Maureen and asked her to pray that I would find this man and that God would show me what to say to him. "Before you called," she answered, "in my mind's eye, God had already shown him to me. He's filled with sorrow. He feels lost, and he's crying out to God. He needs you to find his heart."

"How will I recognize him when I see him?"

"You'll just know him when you see him."

So I looked for him in Australia, but I didn't find him there. I flew on to New Zealand, and he wasn't there either. Two months later, I spoke at a conference on the Father's love in Bad Vöslau, Austria. As one of the other speakers took the microphone, I felt drawn toward a dark, cavernous hallway at the back of the auditorium. There I spied a twenty-one-year-old with soulful, yearning eyes, standing alone in the shadows, listening wistfully to happy stories about how others had found the Father's love. Instantly, I felt a deep love for him. I knew he was the one.

"What is your name?" I asked.

"Thomas."

"Thomas, may I pray for you?"

He consented, and I prayed that Jesus would absorb into His cross whatever pain Thomas could not bear, and that his heart could receive the blessings God had in store for him.

That night an unexpected visitor sailed into my hotel room uninvited—right through a locked door! He was tall, somewhat emaciated, and nearly naked. His feeble back was hunched over like a tied-down sapling. His slate-gray skin exuded the death that was balled up in the dark, dismal recesses of his soul. Normally, I see demons only in my mind's eye, but this one was plainly visible in the bleak light of the streetlamp in the town square outside my window. I sensed it was perturbed that I was on the verge of interfering with its unholy scheme—to fuse its decrepit spine with that of Thomas and slowly and insidiously disintegrate the moral backbone he would need for the work God would lay out for him. In the name of the strong Lion of Judah, I cast it from my room and prayed for Thomas' protection.

I am not an impulsive man by any means, but the following evening in front of seven hundred people, I asked this young man I had met only the day before to be my spiritual son! Thomas consented, and while the audience stretched out eager hands toward him in prayer, I melted into a mortified puddle of self-doubt. "Dear Lord, what have I done? I don't even know this kid! Was I just shamelessly promoting myself? Did I need the audience to be impressed with me?"

Perhaps to keep me from becoming too self-assured, God waited a few years to answer these questions. Eventually, my embarrassment faded as I came to realize that whatever my subconscious motives might have been, God had, in His grace, used my actions for His purposes. I hoped that God meant what I did as a kind of prophetic act, a summons to my generation to call forth lost youths beset by strength-stealing principalities and help them gain the fortitude we had failed to build into their hearts. To be sure, it was a way to get me to state my commitment to Thomas in the presence of a crowd of witnesses to whom I was accountable to keep it. And so, for the last thirteen years I have talked with Thomas online weekly from my side of the Atlantic, praying for the healing of his soul, calling his inner man to rise up in strength, and coaching him through two job failures and a romance that ended painfully. Today, I see standing before me an emerging leader, fueled with God-inspired zeal, studying for the ministry, newly married to a lovely, effervescent German girl named Esther who had been a worship-leader in her church.

In my mid-forties, several years before I met Thomas, friends my age began noticing that many of his generation were coming into the full bloom of their ministries earlier and with greater ease than we ever had. Although we had done well enough in ministry, we sensed that we had been partially held back and that we still had much unrealized potential.

"Why?" I prayed.

"To learn to become wise and loving elders, the spiritual fathers and mothers our culture lacks," the Holy Spirit's still, small voice replied.

I sensed in my spirit that around the time I turned fifty-seven, many of my generation would begin to come into the fullness of our calling, and that this would accelerate during my sixties and into my seventies (at this writing, I am sixty-six). At fifty-seven I did, in fact, begin to discover that fullness. Since then, I have asked audiences around the world if they, too, have begun to discover it: "How many of you have found that in recent years, young people have been drawn to you like a magnet, wanting you to mentor them?" At times, nearly everyone my age and older has raised their hands, as well as a few younger ones.

Years before, I had seen foreshadowings of this. Like the time I switched planes in Denver, coming back from a ministry trip to Florida, and sat down next to a young man from Kentucky named Mark.

"Are you Mark Sandford?" his father asked from the seat beyond him. "Yes! How do you know me?"

"I recognize you from the picture on your ministry's website. We tried to sign up my son for counseling with you, but you're booked up, so we're taking him to the Healing Rooms in Spokane instead." Apparently, God had other plans. Of all the dates on which they could have flown, and all the flights they could have booked, and all the seats on my particular flight, my seat just "happened" to be the one next to his son's! I counseled Mark right there on the plane. In the years since, I have continued to provide him with fatherly counsel and mentoring.

Young men and women keep coming to our door, wanting from Maureen and me what their parents failed to impart. Or, like Thomas, they have needed us to help open their hearts to what their parents had done their best to give, but they could not fully receive, for lack of inner healing. These youths are desperate to make a stand for Christ in an age of compromise, but many lack the solid grounding that comes from the two-parent homes in which most of my generation were raised. When they vowed "for better or for worse," they meant what they said. That's not the world many of these children have known.

At Jasha's fourteenth birthday party, Maureen and I looked around at a dozen of his friends. Only two of them had parents who had not divorced at least once. "Maureen," I said, "divorce has become so common that we never even hear the phrase, 'broken home,' like we used to. It doesn't even occur to people anymore that children whose parents have divorced need sympathy." I looked at the two kids whose parents had stuck it out no matter what struggles they had to endure. They had inscribed eternal truths on their children's hearts; these kids knew from experience that love doesn't change when feelings change. For them, the Bible verse, *"Love never fails"* (1 Corinthians 13:8), was written on pages of flesh. The rest had only the words on paper to guide them.

Deep compassion for the next generation welled up in my heart. "How can they make it through?" I asked Maureen. "They need someone to show them what commitment looks like. Our generation doesn't know what that is." I could envision a vast army of demons like the one that had gone after Thomas, slinking into young people's bedrooms. Poking at their spiritual backbone. Probing for weak spots. Cackling in delight at their parents' negligence. Fusing their own decrepit spines to the compromise that saps passionate, youthful resolve.

I thought again about that passage in Malachi: *"Behold, I will send you Elijah the prophet before the coming of the great and dreadful day of the Lord. And He will turn the hearts of the fathers to their children, and the hearts of the children to their fathers, lest I come and smite the earth with a curse."* And I found myself asking, "Where are you, Elijah? We need you now more than ever."

I realized that if we are to learn to cooperate with Elijah's efforts to turn the hearts of fathers to their children, it will help to understand how he accomplished this in his own generation. I picked up my Bible, turned to 1 Kings 18, and began reading about Elijah at the end of a three and a half-year drought on the dry, shriveled summit of Mt. Carmel. And I imagined what his saga might have looked like through the eyes of someone who was there ...

CHAPTER 5

Elijah's Wake-Up Call

THE SUN SLOWLY ASCENDED in a dusty steel-blue sky, bearing down ever more fiercely on the back of Tobias'* crimson neck as he incessantly dabbed his sweat-streaked brow with a square of tattered muslin. Parched and craving a draft of cool well water, he couldn't bear to lift his eyes to the brittle branches and brown hillsides that disappeared precipitously into the amber haze. But not for a moment did he regret the steep, unforgiving hike to the top of Mt. Carmel. Three and a half years without a sniff of rain has a way of numbing you to the hardships you must endure in your quest for relief.

As Tobias shielded his eyes from the blinding sun, the endless droning by Baal's and Asherah's eight hundred and fifty prophets lulled him into a trancelike state, numbing the futility of it all, muffling their shrill cries: *"O Baal, answer us!"* (1 Kings 18:26 NIV). Tobias glanced up for a moment. They were still gyrating around their altar, frantically prophesying abundant rain and prosperity. After three and a half years of rationing water, gleaning what he could from withered crops, and watching his skin slowly sink between his ribs, these religious fits looked to Tobias like so much childish nonsense. He shut his eyes in disgust and shoved it all to the dusty horizon.

---

* Tobias is a fictional character.

"SHOUT LOUDER!"

Tobias was jolted out of his trance. Elijah wasn't any louder than Baal's frenetic banshees, but somehow his voice seemed amplified, as if blaring from an invisible megaphone in the heavens. *"SURELY HE IS A GOD! PERHAPS HE IS DEEP IN THOUGHT, OR BUSY, OR TRAVELING. MAYBE HE IS SLEEPING AND MUST BE AWAKENED!"* (1 Kings 18:27 NIV).

Tobias was now fully alert. For the first time in his life, he felt real meaning in the precept that while Baal sleeps all winter (temporarily dies, in fact),[1] Yahweh never sleeps. Baal's "prophets" shrieked ever more loudly, slashing their scalps with long, razor-sharp knives (vs. 28). The spurting blood didn't bother Tobias much. The years had accustomed him to the vulgar antics of Baal worship. But he'd had it with their empty promises of mutton in every pot.

"Come here to me," Elijah beckoned (1 Kings 18:30 NIV). The crowd swarmed around him; at this point they would follow anyone who might offer any modicum of relief. The shrieks and cries died away until all Tobias could hear was the clicking of stones, one for each of the twelve tribes of Israel (vs 31), as Elijah piled them up into a makeshift altar. How pathetic it looked next to Baal's magnificent edifice! On this mountaintop—the high place of this austere god—it was believed that he commanded the weather with a lightning bolt held fast in his muscular grip.[2] For his followers, nothing but the most monumental structure of finely dressed stone could merit this hallowed place. Yet somehow, Elijah's little pile of rocks arose with far more dignity.

"Fill four large jars with water and pour it on the offering and on the wood," he commanded (1 Kings 18:33 NIV). Tobias' throat went dry at the sight of that clear liquid refreshment. Where did Elijah get it? Was it rare and precious drinking water?!! For a few moments, the crowd stared incredulously, as if Elijah had commanded them to dump

a fortune in gold off the side of a ship. Nevertheless, they obeyed; once and for all, they would find out which god truly held the power.

"*... Do it again. ... Do it a third time*" (1 Kings 18:34–35 NIV). After the thirsty ground had swallowed its share, water filled the trench dug around the altar. *"Lord, the God of Abraham, Isaac and Israel, let it be known today that You are God in Israel and that I am Your servant and have done all these things at Your command. Answer me, Lord, answer me, so these people will know that You, Lord, are God, and that You are turning their hearts back again"* (vss. 36–37).

A hush fell over the crowd as heads turned skyward. Could it really happen? Through a long, pregnant silence they stood. Transfixed. Waiting. Wondering.

Suddenly, a roaring gust of red and orange wildfire exploded downward upon Elijah's altar! Tobias shielded his face from the heat of the searing blast. In a blinding instant it burned up the wood and the sacrifice and rapidly consumed even the stones, the water, and the soil around the altar (1 Kings 18:38)!

... Then it died away as quickly as it had appeared.

The crowd stood motionless, mouths agape, all eyes fixated on a blackened crater belching a lone, curling wisp of gray smoke. Next to it rose an impeccably carved, shining set of stairs leading up to an imposing altar laden with a half-dried carcass swarming with the flies that symbolized Beelzebub—the "Lord of the Flies." The silence was broken only by a faint, distant breeze rattling a few dry leaves clinging to brittle branches.

Then, in perfect unison the people fell as one, faces to the ground, and roared, *"THE LORD—HE IS GOD! THE LORD—HE IS GOD!"* (1 Kings 18:39 NIV).

Elijah stepped forward with both the humility of a servant and the bearing of a newly crowned king. He commanded the Israelite men,

"SEIZE THE PROPHETS OF BAAL!" and ordered them to take them to the Kishon Valley to be executed (vs. 40).

On the long downhill trek, Elijah's fire began to burn away the debris that had buried Tobias' brittle heart. "I have served Baal for years, for nothing!" His thoughts drifted back to his first year of marriage when he and Mara were called on to offer the ultimate sacrifice to gain Baal's favor.

His heart began to sink.

Tobias had wrested his first-born son from Mara's quaking hands and solemnly marched into the hot, sweaty bowels of Baal's temple where he ceremoniously handed the child over to the high priest. The priest then carried him slowly, solemnly, up the stairs to the gigantic brass statue of Baal—a looming mass of human muscle with the head and horns of a bull, perched pompously on a massive throne of stone. From his toes to the tips of his horns he shone blood-red in the dark, murky expanse, heated to glowing by the raging fire stoked within his hollow chest. A line of drummers pounded in rapid staccato to drown out the wailing of the mothers outside and to numb the hearts of the fathers to their wives' anguish as the high priest placed their infants, one by one, in Baal's glowing, outstretched hands. Tobias' and Mara's little one grimaced, shrieked, convulsed against the searing metal, rolled off into the flames below, and was gone forever.[3]

"What have I done?" Tobias whimpered. "My God, my God, what have I done?"

As Tobias slipped and stumbled down the stiff, dry grass toward the valley below, dying embers of conscience burst into flame. Images flooded his mind—of the deadness that crept into Mara's eyes as, for nine months, she braced her heart for that inevitable, gruesome moment. Of her downcast face each time Tobias returned from the "holy" prostitutes at Baal's temple.[4] Of the confusion in her eyes about how such duties could be called "sacred" when they only drove her and Tobias apart. (Although she had never dared to say it, Tobias knew she felt that his heart was with them, not her.) Of the sorrowful yearning in his children's eyes when his heart had grown so cold that, even in their presence, he no could longer bring himself to be present for them.

"What have I done to my family?"

In the naked light of conscience, Tobias could now clearly see how hideous was the god he had slavishly served for so many years. Every year, when Baal would awaken in the spring, like a celestial porn addict he would gaze lustfully upon Tobias and a host of other fools fulfilling their "sacred duty," cavorting with the temple's "holy" prostitutes. Baal would then turn to his wife (who was also his mother), the goddess Asherah, and pour out his incestuous lust upon her.[5] His seed would then wet the earth in the form of raindrops.[6] Generations of men had been duped into believing that whoremongering and the savage murder of their children had saved their families from famine and poverty. For the first time, Tobias cringed at how truly wretched it had been to stand in the rain, soaked to the skin by one of Baal's "cloudbursts." He felt a stirring in the back of his throat. He wanted to vomit.

"All for nothing!" he muttered through clenched, bared teeth. "This whole thing's been for NOTHING!"

Tobias marched onward, more ready than ever to put to death the influences that had hardened his heart toward his family and dragged the nation into the grips of the horned red king of darkness. He marched on, ready to comfort his wife and beg his children's forgiveness.

"Lord, help me," he pleaded. "Help me turn my heart back to my children. Lord, help us all. Please forgive us. Take away the suffering of our land under this horrible curse."

… And then the rains came.

1 John H. Walton, Victor H. Matthews, & Mark W. Chavalas, *The IVP Bible Background Commentary, Old Testament,* (Downers Grove, IL: Intervarsity Press, 2000), 377 (section on 1 Kings 17:22).

2 "Canaanite Gods and Goddesses," *American Bible Society,* Accessed February 23, 2021, bibleresources.american.org/resoursce/Canaanite-gods-and-goddesses.

3 "Did the Canaanites Really Sacrifice Their Children?", *Bible Reading Archaeology* (May 13, 2018), Accessed February 12, 2021, https://biblereadingarcheology.com/2016/05/13/did-the-canaanites-sacrifice-their-children/.

4 "Baal," *New World Encyclopedia,* Accessed Feb 6, 2021, newworldencyclopedia.org/entry/baal.

5 "Fertility and Vegetation Cults (In the Bible)," *Encyclopedia.com,* Accessed February 2021, https://www.encyclopedia.com/religion/encyclopedias-almanacs-transcripts-and-maps/fertility-and-vegetation-cults-bible.

6 Eugene H. Merrill, *Kingdom of Priests* (Grand Rapids, MI: Baker Publishing Group, 2008), 180.

CHAPTER 6

John the Baptist —
in the Spirit and Power of Elijah

BAAL LOST HIS PLACE on Carmel that day, but there were always diabolical schemes to fall back on. He knew his own true nature, which St. Paul would later reveal: *"The sacrifices of pagans are offered to **demons**, not to God"* (1 Corinthians 10:20, emphasis mine). Baal and his fellow "gods" were mere demons, subject to their leader, Satan. If they could deceive Yahweh's people into partnering with them, then people would become just like demons, for, *"Those who make [idols] will be like them"* (Psalm 115:8).

Eight centuries after Elijah's showdown with the false prophets, God raised up another "Elijah"—John the Baptist—to turn His people back to Himself once again. St. Luke alluded to Malachi 4:5-6, saying of John: *"It is he who will go as a forerunner before Him in the spirit and power of Elijah, to turn the hearts of the fathers back to their children, and the disobedient to the attitude of the righteous, so as to make ready a people prepared for the Lord"* (Luke 1:17). By then, Baal was no longer able to entice the Jews to worship his statue. But this was no great loss to him. There were other ways to convince hapless fools to sacrifice their babes—and just as effective. Statues were never the point. Idols don't have to look like statues.

I close my eyes and picture John by the banks of the Jordan. I imagine a young man named Tobias* arriving on a clear, cool morning. Although blind to his own idolatry, he had always felt a passion to become like his ancestor, Tobias the humble (after whom he was named) who, on that fateful afternoon with Elijah atop Mt. Carmel, was convicted of his idolatry, repented, and remained uncompromising, even after the nation of Israel resumed its trek toward destruction.

Tobias sprinted to the end of a rapidly growing line of people waiting to be baptized. At that moment, John began to scold the Pharisees and Sadducees: *"YOU BROOD OF VIPERS!"* Tobias found it shocking that a man of peace would shout such blunt words! Yet even when speaking so sternly, John's eyes were filled with tender concern. *"Who warned you to flee from the coming wrath? Produce fruit in keeping with repentance. And do not think that you can say to yourselves, 'We have Abraham as our father.' I tell you that out of these stones God can raise up children for Abraham"* (Matthew 3:7–8).

"What is he saying?!!" thought Tobias. "That being sons of Abraham gives us no righteous merit? That makes us no better than Gentiles!" He had expected something like the ritual baths Jews took before entering the temple courts. John's baptism sounded more like the bath a gentile took to wash away his pagan nature and become a Jew. As a Pharisee, the thought repulsed Tobias. Almost out loud, he fumed, "I am a Hebrew of the highest order!" But after a few moments' consideration, he resolved that feigning lowliness would be a noble gesture and a chance to model humility to persons of lesser moral stature.

---

* Tobias is a fictional character.

As the line crept along at a painfully slow pace, Tobias grew impatient for his turn to be baptized. Surprisingly, that desire faded in the light of the Baptist himself. For brief moments, through the dense crowds, John's radiant face popped in and out of view. He both fascinated and frightened Tobias. "Why do I feel like running away?" he asked himself. And yet he couldn't pull himself away. He craned his neck this way and that, hoping to catch another glimpse of John. Something was drawing him toward the river, as if an unseen force was tugging at the hem of his mantle. "I can't go down there right now," he thought. "I'll lose my place in line."

At last, Tobias could no longer resist, and he made his way toward the river. The closer he came, the more he felt driven forward. Finally, he cast aside all etiquette and rudely squeezed through densely packed bodies until he stood knee-deep in the muddy current, a stone's throw away from what felt to him like the center of the universe.

From a distance, Tobias had sensed the spellbinding glow of a raging fire. Close up, he saw a man—just a man. The "fire" didn't emanate from John. It was heaven's light, illuminating something like a peaceful mist that Tobias could almost inhale. A heavy woolen blanket of urgent conviction rolled over the crowd and hushed every voice except John's. In the intense silence, Tobias couldn't help but stare at his face—the gentlest, most humble he had ever seen, yet radiant with the fiercest authority and resolve he had ever witnessed.

Tobias glanced over at a fellow Pharisee from his village. He had always admired this man—a fountain of immense knowledge, a man of dignity and prestige. But in the ambient light of John's humility, he looked like a little boy feeling lost, wishing someone would tell him how important he was. Tobias detected a flicker of envy in the man's eyes and thought, "Something tells me this man wishes he could stand in John's place, and that he secretly hates him for it."

The man thrust his jaw forward and chided, *"Why then are you baptizing, if you are not the Christ, nor Elijah, nor the Prophet?"* (John 1:25). Tobias' heart sank. It was true; John had just admitted he was none of these (vss. 20–21). He looked back anxiously at John.

John answered with grace far more palpable than the arrogance of the Pharisee. He said not a word in his own defense but deferred to the One who would hold the greatest of these titles: *"Among you stands One whom you do not know. It is He who comes after me, of whom I am not worthy to untie even the strap of His sandal"* (vss. 26–27). John words went forth with authority birthed from humility.

A deep witness welled up in Tobias. "If this is what it feels like to be in the presence of John," he thought, "what must it feel like to be in the presence of the Messiah for whom he is a forerunner?" Tobias looked back at the Pharisee; he was scowling like a petulant child. Tobias looked again at John; his manly face was a portrait of gracious Father God. No matter what his fellow Pharisees thought of John, Tobias could not deny that through him, heaven had visited earth.

Tobias' thoughts drifted back to a day when an acquaintance nearly drowned. After his close brush with death, he had told his circle of friends that he could hardly bear to step away from the doorway to paradise and return to his loved ones. Tobias now understood what he had meant. He could have stood on the edge of that river forever. The look in John's eyes was the look in the eyes of this man's closest friend as he dragged him from the water, cradled him in his arms, and pled with God for his life. Tobias had never seen a look so tender. He looked back at the Pharisees. They were in a spiritual stupor; they didn't even know they were drowning. But for the first time in his life, Tobias knew that he was.

The Pharisees feigned humility while strutting like matrons at a gala for the upper crust, each vying to convince the guests that hers were the most glamorous jewels. They basked in the pallid glow of their own intellects, but John's simple words illuminated the world. The wealthy he baptized began to give far more than their excess to the poor. Roman soldiers began acting like lawful Jews. Even money changers had an awakening of conscience and stopped cheating their own countrymen (vss. 12–14)!

But it was what John preached about the family that awakened Tobias' conscience. Before John's birth, an angel had announced to his father, Zechariah, that he would come in the spirit and power of Elijah, and, as Malachi had prophesied, would *"turn the hearts of the fathers back to their children"* (Luke 1:17). As John unfolded Elijah's mandate, Tobias reflected on the endless hours he had spent polishing his jewels with the haughty "matrons" of Israel's pious elite. For the first time, he realized where he had invested all his love, and thought, "What did that ever do for my family?" His children no longer ran into his arms when he came home from his religious soirees. When he walked in the door, he had little love left for them. He had spent it all displaying to the ordinary folk what a superior son of Abraham he had become.

"I never saw how self-focused I am," Tobias whispered to himself. He stared at his feet remorsefully and mumbled, "But my children have noticed." Tobias' noble ancestor and namesake, that great yet humble Tobias, had descended from Mt. Carmel knowing he was an idolater who had sacrificed his child to Baal to serve himself. Now, Tobias left the Jordan knowing he was no different. "He sacrificed his child to make the rains come," thought Tobias. "I sacrifice mine to make myself look spiritual."

Tobias embarked on the journey home with far more resolve than when he had traveled to the Jordan. He would return to the river another day to be baptized by John. For now, he would bring forth fruits in keeping with repentance.

And he would feed those fruits to his love-starved children.

CHAPTER 7

Baal's Strategy for Our Time

MORE THAN TWENTY-EIGHT CENTURIES had passed since Tobias' awaking of conscience on Mt. Carmel, and more than twenty since his descendent and namesake, Tobias, had his reckoning at the Jordan. Baal knew that what worked then would not work in the twenty-first century. A new strategy was needed for a new era. He leaned on the armrest of his false but massive throne and took a few moments to relish his laurels before contemplating his options.

"The Baptist is gone. But I am still here." Baal sat up, proudly thrust out his chest, and smoothly swiveled his bullish head from side to side, surveying the masses of humanity as if they were all his very own possession. "I … am … still … here," he said again, pompously savoring every word, although he knew no one could hear him. "I am *always* here," he pronounced triumphantly. "And you don't even know it!" He tossed his head back and rolled his eyes. "Maybe if you morons would read your Bibles once in a while. Even when you do, you're too dull to see me in it!" Baal let out a childish giggle. In a mocking voice, he quoted 1 Corinthians 10:20: *"The things which the Gentiles sacrifice, they sacrifice to demons, not to God."* He continued the verse in a higher pitched, sing-song cadence: *"And I do not want you to become partners with demons!"* He lowered his voice to a soft growl. "Tell *that* to the myriads of souls—ha! even Christian souls—who think I'm nothing more than an archaic bit of Bible history!"

Again, he stated, this time with a prolonged, snake-like hiss: "I ... am ... sssstill ... here." He grinned and snickered like a giddy little boy who had robbed the piggy bank in plain view of everyone and gotten away with it time and time again.

Baal's thoughts drifted back to the happy years before Elijah's moment of triumph. "There was a time when people knew who I was. I was a GOD! They called me by name! They worshipped ME!" Baal snorted, closed his eyes, and drew a long, deep breath through the blunt, furry snout between his twisted horns. In his thoughts, he was back in his temple in the grand old days, basking in the spotlight of the people's adulation. Softly he exhaled his words: "Awww. All those little ones." He pictured their tiny naked bodies writhing in his huge, red-hot hands. For an endless moment Baal sat. Motionless. His powerful chest heaving drawn-out, bottomless breaths. He closed his eyes, took one last deep breath, tossed back his head, and expelled in an explosive whisper the word, "ECSTASY!"

Baal snapped out of his dark meditation, and his serene face fell into a scowl. "Why did *He* have to show up?" he snarled. "Everything was going so well. It wasn't enough to take away my worship and get them to worship Him. That loathsome creature made Himself one of *them!*"

For a moment, Baal managed to haul himself out of his self-pity and turn his thoughts toward one of his most pleasant memories. Like a loose woman fondly reminiscing about a guilty pleasure, he crooned in a soft, high-pitched voice, "He died the most delightful death." Gleefully, Baal envisioned the little man nailed to the crossbeams, writhing against the splintery grain that scraped His gaping wounds. A tepid smile stretched across his bared teeth.

Reality wiped it off his face. "Suddenly I've got a thousand little Elijahs rising up against me. NOBODIES! And He gave them *His* power! All they have to do is invoke His abominable name, and they can expel my most glorious minions." He clenched his razor-sharp teeth. "Who do they think they are? Pathetic little NOTHINGS!"

Baal propped his elbow on the arm of his dark throne, perched his chin on his white-knuckled fist, and impatiently rapped his fingers on the opposite armrest. "What to do? ... What to do?" On any other occasion, he would have reveled in prizes already won. Perverse sexual delights broadcast into homes worldwide; millions sacrificing their unborn children, calling to memory the bountiful gifts of newborns from the Canaanites—and all to his glory! But at that moment, he was focused on another tantalizing prize—the people the Messiah calls His own.

"I've got to get *Him* out of the way," Baal growled. "What enticements might lure feeble little minds away from Him?" Idols of wood and stone were out of the question. "Too obvious and archaic." He knew that no one would fail to recognize the evil behind them. And in the permissive culture of the modern world, religiosity like that of the Pharisees of John the Baptist's era held little appeal.

Then, a sly grin crept across Baal's devilish face. "Yessss," he hissed, exhaling the word in a breathy voice as if savoring the most relaxing shoulder massage. "Yessss ... that's it. Take all the pain out of it. Don't make them squirm as they watch the flames devour their screaming brats. And don't expect them to slave away, logging long hours of religious studies under their teacher's watchful eye. No; this time let them feel nothing but enjoyment. And let them worship their beloved Jesus while they're at it! Let my all-encompassing cloud descend upon their befuddled hearts and minds. Let it caress their naive little souls until a new 'Christ' appears. Let it be a *nice* Christ," Baal crooned as if petting the cutest little puppy. "A lion without claws. A Christ who offers 'virtue' without discipline. 'Love' without commitment. And above all..." Baal drew in a long, deep breath, then slowly and sensuously breathed out the words: "grace ... without ... repentance."

His leathery lips curled into a jagged smile. "None of that morose 'take up your cross' nonsense! Make them feel *goooood*. Let nothing get in the way of that. Not even concern for their beloved little ones. Let a cloud of self-love descend upon their impressionable souls. Let it put that insipid sentiment to sleep. Deep … restful … sleep."

Baal closed his serpentine eyes and basked in the sweet prospects of these tantalizing dreams. "There's more than one way to get humans to sacrifice their precious progeny! Let them become so self-absorbed that they can no longer see beyond themselves. No more milk and cookies for you, my dear little ones; your elders will be engrossed in far more noble pursuits." The thought so elated Baal that he momentarily forgot he had uttered the very name he most despised. He laid back his massive head, let out a long, dreamy sigh, and was transported to a realm infused with a kind of intoxicating rapture that only demons would dare to call "joy."

A pale, blue-gray mist materialized in Baal's lap, spilled over his knees and, in snakelike cadence, poured slowly down the massive stone steps descending from his throne. As it reached the base of the stairway, it wafted upward. The steamy haze gathered into billowing clouds and morphed into a dark, massive thunderhead that leaned ominously toward the broad expanse of humanity in the distance.

"Yessss," he said with a blissful, Mona Lisa smile. "Yessss … Let *that* be their undoing."

CHAPTER 8

The Cloud Descends

"I HAVEN'T SEEN HER in three years."

"Why not?" I asked incredulously.

"She wouldn't answer my calls."

"Have you sent any text messages?"

"Yeah, but she ignores them."

"Have you sent letters?"

"Yeah, but she didn't answer."

Our conversation had begun as a discussion of the things of God. Shane* had regaled me with stories of incredible miracles and the spiritual gifts he was discovering, and how he had eagerly attended every prophetic conference within a day's drive. His eyes brightened as he shared the highlights—the rush he felt as thousands lifted their hands in prayer, the prophecies that a revival would turn our nation around! But as soon as I asked about his daughter, the excitement faded.

"Are you still going to call or write her anyway?" I asked.

"What's the use? Like I said, she won't answer."

"Have you tried to visit her in person?"

"If I go to her door, I'm afraid she won't let me in."

"But have you gone to her door?" (I hoped I didn't sound like I was prying.)

---

* "Shane" is a composite of several persons.

"Well … no."

A cloud seemed to hover over Shane's mind. I peered into his eyes. The fire I had seen there moments before was dying. Silently, I asked the Holy Spirit for wisdom about what to say next.

"Shane, why do you think she shut you out?"

"She said it was something I'd failed to do. I'm not sure what it was; she wouldn't say. But I do understand why she'd be angry. When she was little, I was too busy with work, and when I came home at night, I sat and watched football most o' the time."

"I wonder if, in her silence, she's sending you a message. Maybe she's trying to get you to pursue her?"

"Ummm … nah," Shane replied after barely a moment's reflection. "I don't think so. She just shut me out of her life."

A Christian news program was blaring from the next room: "A recent survey reveals that young people are leaving the church in record numbers." For a moment, it distracted Shane; then he refocused on my questions.

"How long did you try to reach out?" I asked.

"About six months."

"How *often* did you reach out?" (By now, I was hoping I didn't sound like an interrogator.)

Shane was growing irritated at the noise from the next room: "Our correspondents asked some of the nations' top Christian leaders how we can reverse this trend. Their answers were varied—"

"Darla! Would you turn that down? I'm trying to hear what Mark is saying!" He turned back to me and struggled to regain focus. "I tried calling her three times. She didn't answer. Then I wrote a letter, but she didn't answer that either."

By now, the embers in Shane's eyes were just about extinguished. I imagined the yearning in the eyes of the father of the prodigal son as he watched for him to return home. He must have been a wealthy man, for only such a one could have seen over the village wall as his son approached on a distant hill. (The poor lived in one-story hovels, but the wealthy often lived in two-story villas higher than the city wall.)[1] How many months or even years had he waited on the roof, peering over the wall, watching for his son, never knowing whether he would return? There was no phone or mail service through which to contact him. All he could do was watch and pray. But at least he reached out in that way—the only way he could. And he never gave up. The fire in his eyes never went out. It was this fire that greeted his returning son and melted his heart.

But Shane had given up.

"Shane," I said, "I'm not sure, but I think I might be sensing that your daughter is testing you. She wants you to keep sending letters and text messages until you've proven you'll never stop pursuing her. She may be acting like she doesn't want you, but I suspect she secretly wants you to earn her trust." The flicker in Shane's eyes wasn't getting any brighter.

I shared a few words about the Prodigal Son's father. By now, I could tell that Shane was just patiently enduring my comments. I sensed I was on the verge of sounding preachy, so I left him with a simple admonition: "Try again, and don't give up. Eventually, she'll come around." Shane looked ever-so-slightly relieved that our conversation on that subject was over. He switched to a lighter topic, and our chat wound down. He showed me to the door, said his goodbyes, politely excused himself, and went off to attend to some business of his.

As the door swung shut, I could hear the news show faintly continuing: "Pollsters say that if present trends continue..."

I thought of several parents like Shane whom I had gently challenged. Their prodigals had turned their backs on them, and they had given up pursuing them. Years had passed with no further effort to reach out. One man told me he hadn't seen his son in seventeen years and had quit trying fourteen years previously. In his face I could barely detect any regret and not a hint of remorse. And yet, he was asking for prayer and counsel—to help him deal with hindrances to his Christian walk! Long ago, any awareness of this contradiction had disappeared into the cloud, and the embers in his eyes had gone stone-cold. I gently remonstrated with him as best I could, but he returned home as blind as when he had arrived.

"What has happened to these parents?" I thought. "A petulant child says, 'If you don't care about me, I won't care about you.' Don't they know that even if a prodigal never returns, a parent never gives up?"

Most parents aren't nearly as alienated from their children as Shane was. But the state of his heart previewed the end game of Baal's plans. He conjures his cloud to blind us to our children in so many ways, hoping that one day, we might all become like Shane. Since the day my generation dubbed ourselves "the me generation," the same self-absorbed mentality that kept Shane from seeing his daughter's heart has infused the entire culture.

Few parents consciously decide to put their own needs before those of their children. It happens nearly unconsciously, in the smallest increments. In the myriad moments when pain pulls us inside ourselves. In the moments when our needs scream louder than theirs and we attend to the louder voice. Slowly, imperceptibly, the cloud of self-love gathers around us until self-focus becomes second nature. Until it becomes a lifestyle. Satan's messenger whispers into our ears until we perceive his message as the natural flow of life and the normal way of our people. Over a thousand little steps, the cloud descends from the false throne of darkness, lures us into the fog, and lulls us to sleep as a dark thunderhead gathers above.

"Have we forgotten the difference between a parent and a child?" I thought. "We had better remember, or the curse of Malachi 4:5–6 may soon be upon us."

1   Kenneth Bailey, "The Cross and the Prodigal" (Lecture, Denver Theological Seminary, Englewood, CO, April, 1981).

CHAPTER 9

Killing the Spider

I COULDN'T JUDGE SHANE. Not only because the Word of God restrained me, but because I had been just as self-absorbed. Although I never turned away from my children like he had, my heart would not cooperate with my desire to turn toward them. So the makings were there for the father of a prodigal. Thankfully, none of my children became one; they never closed their hearts to me. But that's only by God's grace and their ineffable forbearance.

… And a pesky thorn in the flesh.

I felt the first prick of that thorn in the first year of marriage. I discovered that Maureen had a temper. The slightest irritants ignited explosions in her, which I, in contrast, was able to weather with dignified solemnity.

Or so I thought.

"We need to find the root of your anger and deal with it," I implored her.

"You're no better than me," she snapped. "You're just as angry as I am; you just never show it!"

"I'm not saying I'm better than you," I retorted. "I'm just saying there's a root in you that causes you to be this way. *You're* the one who struggles with anger."

And so it went. For a season, our verbal ping-pong matches never ended with a cure for Maureen's ills. During that time, God never

59

once spoke to me about Maureen. He always spoke to me about me. And not without some rather disturbing prompting. My *"thorn in the flesh,"* which St. Paul dubbed *"a messenger of Satan"* (2 Corinthians 12:7), was not Maureen's temper. It was literally a messenger of Satan.

One night as I drifted off to a pleasant asleep, I was jolted awake and saw that messenger with my very eyes. A demon in the form of a reddish-brown spider was creeping surreptitiously across our bedroom ceiling. It had a body the size of a saucer and a leg-span nearly three times that wide! It startled me, but I wasn't afraid. As a child, my parents had calmly taught me that demons are nothing to be feared. "Even the smallest child can chase a demon away," they promised. "All you have to do is command it to leave in the name of Jesus. He's a thousand times stronger than it is."

"Maybe it's a kind of hallucination," a friend suggested. "In that twilight zone on the way toward falling asleep, you may actually be dreaming while half awake." That seemed plausible, so I tried an experiment. The next time the spider appeared, I waited until I was fully awake before commanding it to leave. ... It was still there. I tried this a few times, sometimes lying fully awake with eyes wide open for well over a minute. Once, I waited for several minutes. Every time, it was still there.

On a few occasions, the spider fell off the ceiling and sailed toward my chest as its body rapidly expanded to the width of a tympani drum. This gave me quite a jolt! But since my parents' teaching was ingrained in my heart, I always managed to send it away just before it could land, and the scare never lasted beyond the moment.

"Why does God keep letting the spider come back night after night?" I thought. Since the Devil is *"the father of lies"* (John 8:44), I asked the Holy Spirit, "What lie, hidden in my heart, is *attracting* this demon?"

A few days later, the answer came in an unexpected way. Maureen quipped about some minor offense (which I can no longer recall). At the end of the day, I unloaded on her: "You've been angry at me over and over all week! All you do is criticize, and you almost never say anything good about me!"

Gently and with tact, Maureen replied, "Remind me, when in the past week did this happen?"

Aside from that one moment of irritation, I couldn't remember a single instance, and not one criticism! I was flabbergasted. There had been weeks when Maureen was critical, but this was not one of them. Maureen reminded me of several compliments she had given me that week. I had to admit, I had forgotten every one of them! I realized she was not the one I was reacting to. I was reacting to something that had happened long ago.

The Holy Spirit directed my thoughts to my eleven-year-old self on a bleak, late-autumn day. "What's wrong with you?!" Mom scolded. At that time, she couldn't have known I was on the Autism Spectrum (formerly called Asperger's Syndrome—many of the symptoms of which, God has graciously cured). Asperger's would not be a widely known diagnosis for another twenty-eight years. There were so many symptoms she couldn't understand. She couldn't know, for instance, that the damaged social region of my brain was nearly incapable of warning me how inappropriate it would be to abruptly inform a dinner guest that her plaid shirt clashed with her striped scarf.

Mom grabbed my arm and forcefully pulled me aside. "Don't you know how that came across? Anyone your age should know better than that! You need to learn to think about what you're saying!"

I dropped my eyes in shame.

"Look at me!" she fumed.

I raised my eyes slightly. Misfiring neurons were making my facial and shoulder muscles jump and twitch in quirky rhythms (Autism Spectrum is often accompanied by symptoms similar to Tourette's Syndrome).

"Look me in the eyes! Don't you know how weird you look when you do that?!"

I raised my eyes to hers, but not the eyes of my heart. After a childhood of misunderstandings, I could no longer see the tender lover of souls who had rocked me and sung to me, tucked me in with bedtime prayers, bandaged my scraped knees, held me till the tears were dry, and said "I love you" countless times with real intent. I couldn't conceive of how to fit both the kind, tender Mom and the harsh, critical Mom into the same world. To make the confusion go away, I decided to believe that the kind Mom was not the real Mom. I didn't decide this consciously. Children rarely think these things through; they just react. Eventually, such reactions become permanent and take on a life of their own.

As the years went by, Mom gradually discovered the principles of inner healing that transformed her into the Proverbs 31 woman of whom it is said, *"The teaching of kindness is on her tongue"* (Proverbs 31:26). She left behind her shaming ways. But my heart didn't leave them behind.

Now, decades later, like St. Paul I cried out, *"I do not understand what I do. For what I want to do is not what I do, but what I hate I do"* (Romans 7:15). I wanted to drink in Maureen's affirmations. But long ago, the lie that a woman's love isn't real had cancelled every compliment my mother—or any woman—would ever lay like a laurel wreath upon my brow. "Forgive me, Lord," I prayed, "for believing the lie that the kind and loving mom wasn't real."

Then I quickly returned to my righteous quest to get at the roots of Maureen's anger. But God granted no insights, and the spider returned to my bedroom ceiling that very night ... and the night after that ... and the night after that.

So, I asked God, "What other lie is my heart still believing?" He showed me, and I repented, then returned to my quest to make

Maureen into a better person. Again, no insights came to me, and again, the spider returned. And again, I asked God to show me the next lie that had cut off my heart from love and life.

Layer by layer, lies were peeled away. Some were related to other things my parents could not have known. Like what happened at age five when I went for a ride with Dad to a house call with a farmer who attended his church. While he and Dad chatted, I sauntered past amber fields of late summer along quaint, white-fenced farms, through the blinking shade of gently swaying weeping willows. I went brimming with verve, scouting for adventure. I returned, a shattered boy yearning for shelter.

My parents could not have known that I had just been gang-raped in a meadow by four teenage farm boys. Smugly, the boys had warned that if I told my parents, they would kill them. They were bluffing; they were just teenagers scaring a little boy into silence. But I didn't know that, so I told my parents nothing. Mom and Dad couldn't know why, overnight, I pulled into a deep, dark cavern, or why I was horrified to let Mom see me naked in the tub. They couldn't know how confused I felt about myself after the rapists bragged about all the things they were going to do to that "pretty little girl." They couldn't know why my personality changed overnight—why I suddenly despised sports and rough play and anything boyish, or why I took a liking to trying on dresses and frilly things. My Mom quickly put a stop to that. But she couldn't know why, as a junior high student, I was still so effeminate that visitors at church would compliment her on what a "charming daughter" she had.

By the time I met Maureen, I had long since reconciled myself with being male, but not with being present in this world. To banish the pain, my heart had made many choices, some consciously and some unconsciously, to disconnect. (In the vocabulary of inner healing, we call these choices "inner vows"). I had vowed not to remember the rape or share the secrets of my heart with anyone. Most of all, not to feel the pain. The pain of hearing the words "faggot" and "queer bait" reverberate through the bustling hallways at school (even though I never gave in to homosexual temptations). The pain of hearing my eighth grade P.E. teacher call me "Suzy" as he mocked my frail body, inciting the entire class to laugh along with him. The pain of hearing Dad tell me I was "like a little girl," forcing me to run up and down stairs as he rode me like a drill sergeant to turn me into a "man." (Again, this was before he had discovered the principles of inner healing and became the wise father so many came to know). The pain of being accused of being weak, even though, as a mere five-year-old, I dared to protect adults from a pack of murderers by choosing to bear the secret of violent gang-rape alone. Forever.

A central principle of inner healing is that our bitter root judgments color the way we see entire classes of persons. To me, all boys were rough and violent. All manly men were insensitive. All women who drew close to me would criticize me. All people would think badly of me. These are all lies, and since Satan is the father of lies (John 8:44), lies attract demons, and the spider found a reason to visit me.

Bitter root judgments make us expect others to hurt us. They magnify hurts and minimize blessings. I tried to numb the pain through inner vows not to feel, not to need, not to trust, not to hope, not to be present, and definitely not to be aware of the deep anger Maureen could sense in my heart.

We make inner vows to make the pain go away. That's a lie; they only make it worse. A deceived heart sends up a cloud that obscures that truth. I could not perceive how profoundly cut-off and self-absorbed my inner vows had made me or how painful that was to Maureen and our children (or even to myself). I had been disconnected from such an early age that it felt normal.

… But every night, the spider reminded me that it was not.

St. Paul urged us to suit up with spiritual armor. Every judgment against others and every inner vow to self-protect is like a piece of counterfeit armor. St. Paul promised that *"the shield of faith"* will *"extinguish all the flaming arrows of the evil one"* (Ephesians 6:16). My shield of bitter root judgments and inner vows extinguished nothing. As I repented of them and forgave those who tempted me to make those judgments and vows, my heart stopped believing lies, and the arrows began to bounce off the godly armor with which I was replacing the counterfeit armor.

After five months of nailing judgment after judgment and inner vow after inner vow to the Cross in prayer, I became more deeply impacted by the gravity of the need for theosis—that lifelong practice of turning to God again and again until the heart becomes a lamp that shines the light of His love. As I kept turning to God, I repeatedly felt His grace, which empowered me to tear down the wall of shame that kept me from seeing my faults. At last, I made a confession to Maureen: "I've realized I'm just as troubled as you are. And just as angry." From that moment on, Maureen felt freer to rise out of the shame that had made looking at her own faults unbearable.

... And finally, God began to reveal the roots of her temper.

Meanwhile, something strangely wonderful had begun to happen. As I persevered in repenting of the many ways I had disconnected from life, the spider began to appear only every other night. Then twice a week. Then once a week. Then once a month. It grew weaker because there was less and less for it to feed upon. I came to understand that when the spider had expanded and sailed toward my chest, it was the lies of my heart, bitter root judgments, and inner vows that had nourished and empowered it to do so. It had wanted to wrap its gangly legs around my chest and squeeze the life out of my heart. But repentance had starved it and stripped it of its power.

When I told my parents about the spider, they were astonished yet not surprised: "We used to see that same reddish-brown spider," they told me, "exactly the same size! Not with our physical eyes like you have, but in repeated visions in our mind's eye. We sensed it was coming against our ministry." That made sense. My parents believed that the main goal of inner healing was to make people whole enough to reconcile with both God and their children. Their trademark verses had always been Malachi 4:5–6: *"Behold, I will send you Elijah the prophet before the coming of the great and dreadful day of the Lord. And He will turn the hearts of the fathers to their children, and the hearts of the children to their fathers, lest I come and smite the earth with a curse"* (NKJV).

I came to realize that I never was the spider's ultimate prey, nor was our marriage. The spider was after our children! It wanted Maureen and me out of the way to get a clearer shot at them. If it could tempt us to close our hearts to each other, the emotional numbness we felt toward each other might dull our hearts toward them. If they reacted to that wounding in the same way I had—by disconnecting from love and life—then the spider could land on them and squeeze the life out of their hearts, too. Why had God opened my eyes so I could literally see the spider? To graphically portray the urgency to seek inner healing through ongoing repentance, and halt a generational cascade of harm.

There came a time when the spider grew so feeble that there was nothing left of it but a faint blob appearing on our ceiling once every six months. It has now been fifteen years since it last appeared. My fight with the spider has ended, yet there is a fight that still goes on. The light that drove that creature of darkness out of our home continues to expose roots of bitterness in my heart and impel me to turn back to Jesus in repentance. Every time I do, He brings more healing to my blinded eyes, so that I may see myself as clearly as I had once seen the spider. And so that I may see the heart of my wife and turn to her in repentance. And so that I may learn to do the same for my children.

I suspect that this work may never be finished this side of heaven. But inner healing is making the emotional anesthesia wear off. As I face my own childhood pain, I am enabled to perceive the pain in my children's eyes. "What's wrong?" I ask them. When they can't find the words, Maureen and I petition God until He makes it clear. And then I apologize ... but I disconnect again. And I apologize again. And again.

... And I become less self-absorbed and more connected.

As our children grew up, sometimes Maureen and I worried that we wouldn't be healed in time to keep them from numbing their hearts. But they always forgave, and they chose to hold their hearts open. Today, as best we can, we continue to repent to them, which helps them choose to forgive. And they continue to forgive as children so often do, as long as their parents try their best. Together, we find our way. And they walk with God in strength and clarity that Maureen and I never knew.

CHAPTER 10

Weathering the Storm for Their Sake

WHAT A BLESSING that our children always choose to forgive! But I don't want to test their patience. So I pray, "Why is it taking so long for me to become the father I've always wanted to be?" I rest my head on the soft cushion of my office chair, close my eyes, and listen for an answer.

… By and by, fathers emerge from the memories of a thousand morning Bible readings. I envision that dreadful evening when Lot cracked open his front door and peered into the darkness. The town's entire male population was clamoring for his male visitors. This insensitive cad offered his daughters (instead of himself) to be gang-raped in their place! Jacob's dad doted on his favorite son Esau but ignored Jacob, tempting him to scheme to steal Esau's blessing. The high priest Eli turned a blind eye to his sons as they seduced women who served at the entrance to the tent of meeting. King Saul pitched a spear at young David to pin him to the wall, paranoid that he'd steal his throne, too blind to see the heart of a loyal spiritual son. David failed to discipline his son, Amnon, for raping his sister, Tamar. This tempted another of David's sons, Absalom, to slaughter his brother Amnon and usurp his father's throne.

"Wow! What a motley collection of dads!" I think to myself. "Are there really that few good fathers in Scripture?" I close my eyes again and ask the Lord to remind me of a few.

I see Abraham. God promised a son, and Abraham waited … and waited. His faith failed; he tried to make it happen on his own, siring Ishmael through his concubine. When the promised son, Isaac, was finally born in his ripe old age, God ordered Abraham to slit his throat on an altar! But when he showed his intention to obey no matter what, God provided a ram in Isaac's place. It took decades to turn Abraham into a good father. Why?

To learn commitment—through a lifetime of patience that taught him obedience at all costs.

I see Joseph, father of Jesus. On the basis of nothing but a dream, he chose to believe the impossible—that his betrothed was a pregnant virgin! He went ahead and married her, allowing the community to suspect that he had sinned with her. He fled to Egypt to keep King Herod from killing the child, then returned to a community that despised him. Why did being a good father have to be so hard?

To show the world an example of commitment—a man who chose to suffer anything for a child yet unborn.

I see Jesus. He raised up twelve spiritual sons. Judas betrayed Him. Peter denied Him. All the rest deserted Him. Only the women and one male disciple, John, stayed with Him at the cross. Jesus *"learned obedience from the things which He suffered"* (Hebrews 5:8). What else did He learn as a spiritual father?

Commitment.

Jesus died the most agonizing death imaginable to save His spiritual children. His commitment enabled us all to do the same for ours.

We tend to think that signs and wonders will inspire the commitment needed for the coming days. The people of Jesus' time were as anxious for signs and wonders as we are, and they got what they wished for. He turned water into wine, fed five thousand with a few loaves and fishes, walked on water, and raised the dead. But none of that inspired the commitment they would need to weather the coming storm. When the going got tough, the crowds hated Jesus as much as they had loved Him.

Even after Jesus rose from the grave, His own disciples' hearts were too dull to recognize who He was. What was the first step He took to open the eyes of their hearts? He sought them out as they hid in fear and shame and, with no condemnation for their betrayal, showed them the scars on His hands and feet—the emblems of His commitment.

Many Israelites were still not convinced that Jesus was the Messiah, even when He showed them proof of His resurrection—the ultimate sign and wonder. What humbled Jesus' disciples and opened their blind eyes was this proof coupled with sacrificial love. This is what finally made way for revival and gave them the strength to endure the storm of persecution that would come with it. His ultimate commitment showed them, as God has shown Maureen and me, that when you know—*really* know—that the Father's heart is with you, you begin to feel joy even in the midst of the storm.

I think of all the young people I've seen swarming to conferences to witness the spectacle of signs and wonders—and how their faith has too often withered when there was a cost of discipleship to be paid. My nephew, a former youth pastor, tells me of young friends of his, youth pastors living with their girlfriends. These are models for a generation that has seen too little of the commitment of uncompromising obedience to God. I wonder how many of their own first models of commitment—their parents—showed more zeal for spiritual experiences than for their children. There is something more than signs and wonders we need to show them. Something far more convincing and motivating.

We need to show them the emblems of our commitment, engraved on upturned palms.

But are we the ones receiving the nails or the ones hammering them? Our children can find it hard to tell the difference when we fail to show them where the culture ends and the church begins. We may disagree with our culture's beliefs, but culture is far more than a set of beliefs. It is more like a pot of spiritual soup. We have been marinating in it for so long that we've slowly and imperceptibly absorbed its most potent flavor: love of self.

Faith has become about me and my wants; the church is a product to be consumed. When worship doesn't please or sermons don't inspire, we shop for a better brand. Signs and wonders are not a clarion call to repentance; they are the glitter and lights for the party. Seldom do we hear Jesus' words preached: *"take up your cross and follow Me"* (Mark 8:34 NLT).

"Prophets" pander to a self-absorbed culture with personal prophecies of health, wealth, and acclaim, while declaring little about the cost of discipleship. Many of them give false prophecy after false prophecy with no retractions or apologies, yet they are still widely reverenced as a mouthpiece of God. As the watchmen sleep on the wall, false teachings creep in. Baal's dark cloud descends while a spider grows larger on the ceiling of the church.

In the last days, when people become *"lovers of self"* (2 Timothy 3:2), only a higher love will counter this. With fondness and gratitude, I look back on a mom and dad who created a culture of commitment in our family. They walked hand in hand for more than fifty years of marriage no matter what they had to work through. Commitment was stamped into my soul through sound teaching, discipline, hugs and kisses, fun and laughter, and milk and cookies. Commitment infused a flavor into the soup that could never be overwhelmed by that of the culture around us. Signs and wonders were common fare in our house, and they impacted us deeply. But it was my parents' self-sacrificial commitment more than miracles that ushered their children into an uncompromising walk with God.

I have spent my life learning to stay on that kind of straight and narrow path, but not without complaint. "Lord," I have prayed, "if I had known what it would take to learn this kind of commitment, I wouldn't have signed up!" Nevertheless, I have come to understand it was more than worth it.

I am reminded of a vision the Holy Spirit painted in my mind's eye at the beginning of our marriage in 1984. Maureen and I would endure a storm. (I'm thankful He didn't tell me how long it would last!) The trials would strengthen us until we became like a rock rising out of the ocean. As our storm would come to an end, the rest of the world would be plunged into its own storm. We would be one of the rocks the next generation would cling to as the waves began to surge—spiritual parents for an increasingly fatherless and motherless generation in danger of drowning.

Facing personal storms without compromise is the cost it will take for our generation to rise to this task. Signs and wonders may attract youth to a revival, but our unwavering commitment to them is what will make its effects last more than one generation. The years have taught Maureen and me that the muscle of commitment needed to accomplish Malachi 4:5–6 is built through a long, strenuous spiritual workout of repentance.

As I look back on my marathon joust with the spider, I am thankful for the commitment that season of theosis built into my soul. In the face of the storm coming upon the world, I now see there was no other way. What took the edge off the struggle is that I was never concerned that the spider might win the battle. Jesus has already *"disarmed the powers and authorities … triumphing over them at the Cross"* (Colossians 2:13 NIV). A conquered enemy can do only that which the conquering general allows. It was God who allowed the spider into our bedroom. That was for His purposes. It got me to put on the spiritual armor of Ephesians 6. It got me to train for war. It made me learn repentance and commitment at all costs.

What St. Paul wrote about the armor of God, he wrote to the entire Ephesian church—and the entire Body of Christ. Everyone is called to wear it and *"take a stand against the devil's schemes"* (Ephesians 6:11). *Everyone's* warfare is *"against rulers, against the powers, against the world forces of this darkness, against the spiritual forces of wickedness in the heavenly places"* (vs. 12). There is only one difference between me and most Christians: God opened my physical eyes to literally witness the warfare that is common to us all.

So many of God's children have assumed that the warfare would be so much easier—God would simply hoist us onto His shoulders and parade us triumphantly past Baal's hideous phalanx of soldiers, straight to the victory celebration. What we didn't count on was how sweaty the training would be.

But Maureen and I are still on the front line. And Gary is here. And hopefully, Shane will join us as the cloud lifts, and he sees his enemy for what he is. And if we are willing to come to grips with how disturbingly self-absorbed our lives have become, Baal's dark cloud may lift off us all. And our hearts will begin to learn what our minds have always known—that as soldiers, we don't put on armor just to protect ourselves. We put it on to express sacrificial commitment; we stand on the front line to protect others.

… For if we are not on the front line, our children soon will be.

Chapter 11

Small Enough to Win the Battle

I STAND ON THE FRONT LINE contemplating the naiveté of my earlier years. I always knew that God had planted a sense of destiny deep within my soul, and I dreamed of the day when it would gloriously unfold. If I was honest enough, I would have to admit that somewhere in the back of my mind I imagined a special platform awaiting me in the pantheon of Christian heroes. Now that I am old, I recoil from such nonsense. The warfare is nothing like what my childish mind imagined it would be. You can't fight while standing tall on a platform. When demons aim their bows, they always aim high, and the humble bow low.

I look around and see the true heroes of this warfare standing on their knees. "Pathetic little nothings," as Baal would call them. Yet, no matter how low they bend in repentance, they have no reason to feel pathetic. How can they feel ashamed of not being big enough to achieve that which was never theirs to achieve? Life's countless skirmishes have beaten back the illusion that there would ever be a platform on which to display their heroics. Or that there even should be, for the Holy Spirit's boot camp is about learning to recognize you're small enough to win the battle. You can never be more than a shepherd with a slingshot. But that's all it takes to bring Goliath down. The dark night, the hard losses, and the patiently endured trials lead to a godly despair of ever growing "big enough" to win.

Gary came to me for counsel, reeling from such despair. "I used to be really awful to my kids," he said with palpable regret. "I never saw that until recently. I was so prideful."

"What do you mean?" I asked.

"My son Jeremy has ADD. He used to get into so much trouble. I did everything I could to stop him. I grounded him constantly. I think he must have spent most of the fifth grade in his room! It never did any good. I'd hear him in there, kicking things, muttering about what a 'jerk' I was. I'd yell at him, 'You be more respectful!' He would shut up, but he'd always come out later with this sour look on his face. One day, Marsha* suggested, 'Why don't you go out and play catch with him for a while?' I was halfway through our playtime before it even occurred to me, this was the first time I'd ever tossed a ball with my son! Then something strange happened. Jeremy wasn't bouncing off the walls anymore! He was totally calm. I'd never seen him that way! All he'd needed to calm him down was some fatherly attention. I've always been an all-or-nothing guy, so that day I decided I'd be the best father I could possibly be. I started playing ball with him as often as I could. But what I don't get is why he still subtly resents me."

"Sounds like there's something he's still not getting from you," I said.

Gary pursed his lips and gave that some thought. "… Yeah, I guess so."

"Close your eyes and ask God what it is."

After a few moments, he opened his eyes, sighed, and threw up his hands. "I've tried to be the best Dad I could be! What else can I do?"

"Gary, did you ever apologize to Jeremy for all the times you hadn't been there to play ball with him before?"

"Well, not for *that* in particular."

---

* "Marsha" is a composite of several persons.

"What have you asked him to forgive you for?"

"Ummm … there was a time when I said, 'If I've ever done anything to hurt you, I'm sorry.'" Gary shrugged. "Didn't seem to make much difference."

How could I wake him up to what he was missing? I stopped to think. "Gary, can you remember a time when your parents made you apologize for something?"

"Yeah."

"What did they make you say?"

"I called my sister, 'fatso,' and they made me say I was sorry."

"What *specific* words did they make you use?"

"I'm sorry for calling you 'fatso.'"

"Did they say anything else?"

"They asked Essie* how she felt. She said I made her feel ugly, and she started crying. That's when I *really* felt bad." Gary shook his head and stated emphatically, "I *never* called her that again!"

I spoke as gently as possible, choosing my words carefully: "Do you see a difference between the way your parents made you apologize to Essie and the way you apologized to Jeremy?"

Gary sat back in his chair and focused his eyes on the wall beyond me. I could tell he had never thought about this before. "… With Jeremy I just said, 'If I ever did *anything* to hurt you.' With Essie I got more *specific* about exactly what I'd done. And my parents made me talk, not just about what I did, but how it made her *feel.*"

I took a moment to make sure there was no hint of judgment in my voice. "How would Essie have felt if you had said to her only what you said to Jeremy: 'I'm sorry if I ever did anything to hurt you'?"

After a long, pregnant pause, Gary sank into his chair as if bracing for an incoming wave. Staring at the floor, he whispered, "No wonder

---

* "Essie" is a composite of several persons.

Jeremy still resents me." He paused to sort out the wave of insights beginning to crash over him. "… I don't think I've *ever* asked him to forgive me for anything *specific*. I just gave one blanket apology."

Gary paused again to let his thoughts catch up with him. "… And I n*ever* asked him how he felt. About *anything*. Especially anything *specific*. I just expected him to forgive me all at once for everything I'd ever done to him and instantly forget all the thousands of hurts he'd ever felt." Gary furrowed his brow, drew in a quick breath, and exhaled. "He had to stuff the hurt his whole life … even after I said, 'I'm sorry.'"

Gary shook his head in disgust. He stared at his feet and lamented, "When I told him, 'I'm sorry,' it wasn't to help *him* feel better. I just felt guilty, and I wanted him to let me off the hook. So *I* could feel better. So *I* could *look* better! It was like, 'Look at *me,* Jeremy; look at what a great father I am.'"

Tenderly I asked, "Gary, whenever you've realized you've hurt people you love, have you ever refused to apologize and make it right?"

"No," he responded in a low voice, still staring at his feet.

I reassured him, "Jeremy knows that. It's not too late."

Gary raised his head and gazed into the distance in rapt silence. Compassion drifted across his face like a mist, softening the hard lines around his watering eyes. He sat for a while, quietly absorbing the revelations like a fresh rain sinking into hard, sunbaked earth. We talked a little longer about what Jeremy's heart needed and what a real apology might sound like. We closed with a prayer that Jeremy could open his heart to receive it.

As a counselor, I had seen that one reason parents don't offer specific apologies is that facing all those dark moments makes them feel small, like they haven't been good parents. But Gary had let go of the illusion that he could become the world's best father, and something in his eyes said it no longer mattered. He had resigned himself to being small enough to win the battle.

I waved Gary goodbye, and he headed home to show Jeremy his scars.

CHAPTER 12

The Gifts of the Magi

EVERY DAY, THE GARYS we counsel pour out their pent-up childhood pain to Maureen and me. Not just the pain of never having heard the words, "I'm sorry," but the pain of never having had a parent listen as they talked out their pain. So we have listened. We have felt with them. But too many have headed back home to utter that vapid one-time apology to their children: "If I ever did anything to hurt you…" Nothing specific in the confession. No listening. No talk of feelings.

As tactfully and gently as we can, we admonish them, "Your children need you to give them what we've given you."

They look dumbstruck. "I can't believe I never thought of that!" they gasp. "It's not that I've refused to. The thought just never crossed my mind." And they don't know why.

These parents aren't being stupid. They just haven't comprehended the real purpose of repentance. They think it's for making themselves into perfect parents. That's why some parents don't utter a blanket one-time apology until they're on their deathbed; only at the last moment do they despair that their perfection is out of reach. And though they have apologized numerous times to God and fellow adults, some never apologize to their kids at all. It doesn't even occur to them to do so. It's not that they don't love their children. They just can't focus on erecting the ideal self and healing their children's hearts at the same time.

As young parents, Maureen and I apologized to our children, but we knew we should do it more often. The problem was, we didn't feel we had the authority to; we didn't think our apologies would sound authentic until we were healed enough to stop hurting them altogether. But time was getting away from us. Jasha was seven, Jonah was ten, and Míchal was thirteen. The teen years were looming ahead of us. If we didn't do something now, our children might not be able to keep holding their hearts open. Despair rose up as it dawned on us that our hope of becoming sufficiently healed might be deferred until they were all well out the door ... if even in this lifetime.

By hindsight, we realize it was a godly despair. You might even call it God's gift of despair, for through it we learned the true meaning of Jesus' words, *"Be perfect, therefore, as your Heavenly Father is perfect"* (Matthew 5:48 NIV). He didn't mean that repentance was a means to build a perfect self. Repentance is turning toward Him who alone is perfect and in whose power we are made perfect. Anything else is an idol. Even perfection.

We came to understand that our children didn't need parents who were committed to pursuing their own perfection. They needed parents who were committed to *them*. They needed parents who were committed to a lifestyle of repentance, who were willing to take up their cross and prove the risen Christ.

A dear old friend, Rose Marie Borelli, knew of our concern for our children. On a cool September afternoon at her home in suburban Chicago, she sat us down on comfy overstuffed chairs, offered steaming cups of lavender tea, and treated us to a video by the late Jack Frost. In a public display of scars, he laid out his sordid past in which he had sacrificed his kids to the dream of becoming the all-time champion swordfish fisherman. Repeatedly, he parlayed his spitfire determination into a catch that was one for the record books, but as these stories go, the triumph was always hollow. It left him with nothing but a fading moment of glory and a gnawing conscience. It dawned on him that he had funneled his steely grit into something other than his children and that the only fire he had spit in their direction was his nasty temper. So, Jack chose to pull down his idol of self-perfection, stretch out his hands, and humbly receive the nails. For three hours he apologized to each of his children through tears and lingering embraces. The next day, a neighbor remarked that Jack's son was able to look her in the eyes for the first time! The shame was off of him, and the scars were on Jack.

That night, Maureen and I sat down to devise a plan for our children. We knew that our brokenness hadn't just hurt them. There were countless times when I was so lost in my brokenness that I inadvertently stole from them. I stole my attention and, in her anguished temper, Maureen stole their peace. We resolved to do for them what our Heavenly Father did for His son. On December 26, we would celebrate a second Christmas and bestow upon them gifts of gold, frankincense, and myrrh, like the three wise men had given to the infant Jesus. As an act of restitution, we would symbolically return what we had taken.

For three months we prepared in prayer. When the morning came, we laid before each of them a little round golden-beige vessel like the ones we had seen in paintings of the wise men, girthed with indented gold stripes and topped with a four-sided pinnacle or a marble-sized half-ball on a domed cap. As snowflakes swirled silently past frost-etched windows, we knelt before our children on a puffy quilt next to a warm fire flickering in our little wrought iron wood stove. We opened the boxes one-by-one and lifted out treasures we had prayerfully selected for each of them.

I clasped a delicate gold chain around Míchal's neck. "Míchal, this cross and necklace are for you because your spirit is pure, like gold."

"Gold is the gift the wise men brought for a king," Maureen said proudly.

I said with gentle authority, "God is going to make you a ruler, because that's what He designed you to be. We see it in the way you lead your friends."

Maureen added, "You're the one who brings all your friends together."

"You're very good at drawing boundaries, too," I said. "You don't let people walk on you, but you also forgive; you give second chances. Your friends respect you for that."

We drew a silver cross on a silver necklace out of Jonah's box, along with a small vial of frankincense. "Jonah," I said solemnly, "frankincense is a gift for a priest, because you minister to your friends."

Maureen recounted fond memories of when Jonah was there for them, shining a light on their path. "You're a shepherd. You know how to make people feel at home, and you show them how to have fun."

"Others want to be like you," I said. "You will give a sense of home to people who've had no home."

For Jasha, there was a silver cross on a silver necklace and a vial of myrrh. "Jasha," Maureen said, "myrrh is a gift of healing."

"The Wise Men gave it to Jesus for His burial," I added. "His death healed us. You're there for other people, like Jesus is. You are very strong for them."

"More than anyone we know, you have a heart of love," said Maureen with admiration. "You're going to bring healing to many people." And so he has. It's what he's known for; whenever a friend is hurting, there is Jasha.

But there was another kind of gift we couldn't fit into those little boxes. We began to lay it out before them.

"Míchal," I said, looking intently into her eyes, "you're able to see what's inside people's hearts. That's something leaders do. You draw out their strengths and raise them up to walk in them. You needed me to do that for you. Do you remember when I went on ministry trips when you were little, and you would make special gifts and hide them in my suitcase?"

"Yeah." Míchal looked a little apprehensive, feeling shy about showing what she felt.

I looked back with deep regret at the little beaded lizards, drawings of flowers in warm-colored crayons, and cutout blue and white paper snowflakes tucked between my folded shirts ... and the letdown in her sad little eyes. So many times, she had waited in suspense to see the delight in my eyes when I scooped her into my arms at the baggage claim. I did, in fact, scoop her up with hugs and kisses, but too often my disconnected heart would fail to remind me of the gifts my little magi had hidden in my suitcase.

"You put a lot of time and work into those gifts, Míchal. And I enjoyed them. But when I got home, I often forgot to tell you how much they blessed me."

Her lower lip began to quiver.

"That's not your fault; those were good gifts. It's not because those gifts weren't a blessing to me. I didn't ignore them on purpose. Sometimes I don't notice things because my heart shut down when bad things happened to me when I was little. I'm seeking help to heal that, so I won't keep doing that to you."

Míchal's own heart had been on the verge of shutting down; I could feel it in her hugs. That wonderful energy that flows from chest to chest was just beginning to fade.

A woman came to mind whom I had recently counseled. "Jeanie"* had grown up under a pounding hail of insults: "Stupid!" "Numbskull!" "Why can't you do anything right?!" Year after year, she had fought to hold her heart open to a mother who never apologized for any of this.

---

* "Jeanie" is a composite of several persons.

Decades later, a little flame of hope still flickered in Jeanie's heart. She stood by her elderly mother's hospital bed, wondering whether in her mother's last hours she would she say something—anything—to show she was aware of the hurt she had inflicted. Her mother reached out and tenderly clasped Jeanie's hand between her own frail, trembling hands and whispered, "If I ever hurt you in any way, I'm sorry."

An hour later, she was gone. Jeanie stood by the bed with one hand resting gently on her mother's folded hands. Frozen in time. Suspended in the stark realization that this is where it all ends.

In the coming months, she sat for countless hours in her mother's rocking chair, sifting through a lifetime of sorrows, laboring to remember the joys. Replaying in her mind that indescribably sweet moment when she heard a once-in-a-lifetime apology, but wishing it was so much more. Wishing she and her mother could have talked out a few of her thousand tearful memories. Trying to make that one moment of apology stretch to cover them all. Begging God to help her hold her heart open to the love her mom hadn't known how to give.

As I looked at the three little innocent faces before me, I silently prayed, "Please help them not to close their hearts. Help Maureen and me to help them talk out their hurts." Míchal was trying her best not to cry, but I could sense her heart was beginning to open—slowly, vulnerably, like a morning glory when it meets the sun.

"When I forgot to thank you for your gifts, how did that make you feel?"

Míchal shrugged and stared back blankly. "I dunno." I knew she didn't really mean that. She knew. What she really meant was, "I'm afraid to show you what I feel, but I want you to come and find my heart." She needed me to speak words that said I could see how she felt. (I am still learning how to do that.)

"Did you feel sad?"

"Yeah," she said softly.

"Did you feel disappointed?"

"Yeah."

"When I came home from trips, you needed me to show how happy I felt about the gifts you gave me. When I didn't, did you feel like you weren't important?"

"Yeah." Míchal could no longer hide the tears.

"Was there anything else you felt?"

"Yeah. … Like you didn't care about all the time it took to make those things for you."

"You really needed me to show what all that effort meant to me. Do you forgive me?"

Míchal nodded and shyly replied, "Yes."

Our children have always said, "Yes." Their hearts never got to be as calloused as mine. I held her as we both cried, until the tears were spent.

At that time, I hadn't yet discovered that some of my disconnectedness was not my fault. I had no way of knowing that a type of petit mal seizures called "absence seizures" (a common symptom of Autism Spectrum) were what caused me to miss portions of conversations. Repeatedly throughout the day, my brain would short circuit and shut off, then turn back on again—sometimes seconds later, sometimes minutes, and I was unaware that I had lost any time.

I remember asking Míchal, "What are you doing tonight?" She bubbled over with excitement, effervescing about all the details of her plans for the evening's get-together with friends. Five minutes later, I asked again, "What are you doing tonight?" Neither she nor I could know that the damaged social region of my brain had failed to record her words and that I had no way of knowing I had missed anything.

Months after our post-Christmas family meeting, we discovered my condition. I told Míchal and the boys, "When you guys hurt each other by accident, we always make you say you're sorry. That doesn't mean you've done anything wrong, does it? It just helps the one you hurt to feel better. So, when my brain blanks out what you say, you still have a right to feel hurt or angry, even if I hurt you by accident. If you're angry, it doesn't mean you're accusing me, and I won't take it personally. It just means you need to say, 'ouch.'"

I would like to think this provided some incentive for the grace my children have given me. What I do know is that when you apologize to children, they forgive a lot more easily than grownups.

"Jonah," I said, "when you were little, there were times when you did something wrong and I made you sit in a corner, but I forgot to tell you when you could get up again." (Short-term memory is a casualty of the ADD that often accompanies Autism Spectrum.) "That must have made you feel like I had forgotten you. That wasn't your fault, Jonah. You didn't deserve that. You deserve to be remembered."

Jonah's large, warm eyes began to soften.

"I never did that on purpose, and I'll always try to improve my memory because I don't want to do that to you. Do you forgive me?"

"Yeah." His eyes were moistening.

"We also snapped at you too often, and you didn't deserve that either."

"I don't remember that," he replied.

Maureen and I knew from experience that while the mind may forget pain—especially in one as tender as Jonah—the heart does not. As children, we had both been snapped at far more severely, and we were rarely allowed to voice the pain. When emotional electricity builds up, how easy it is to turn one of your children into a lightning rod! Often, the tenderest one, the most easily bruised, becomes the scapegoat, and his little flaws are magnified. We never uttered anything like the put-downs Jeanie's mother slung at her. But we suspected that Jonah's sensitive spirit had sensed our subtle irritations. Had they affected his heart as much as we thought? Or were we just being overly careful not to make him the scapegoat we had been when we were children?

In any case, whatever Jonah had done to trigger our anger was so insignificant that Maureen and I could not even recall what it was. But we remembered some of our specific reactions and confessed them to him, because children live and feel in the specific moments of life.

"Jonah," I asked, "Do you believe me when I say that you didn't deserve for us to be angry at you?"

"Yeah."

The sight of Jonah's misty eyes shining out from that kind, gracious little face made me yearn all the more to attune my spirit to his tender heart. We held him close in a long, tearful embrace.

I looked at Jasha, remembering him as a three-year-old on a crisp winter's night. Maureen and I had been fighting in the kitchen in stifled whispers so as not to awaken the kids, and she was crying quietly. Jasha was in his bed—around a corner, through the living room, up the stairs, down a hallway, and behind a closed door. There was no way his little ears could hear us. But his spirit could. We heard tiny footsteps pitter-pattering down the stairs, and before Maureen could finish drying her eyes, little arms were reaching up to her. "I love you, Mommy. I think you're beautiful."

Four years later, seven-year-old Jasha now sat before us, responsible beyond his years. "Jashie, you have a very loving heart," I reassured him. "When your mom is feeling bad, you want to make her feel better. We like that about you; God made you that way! But you don't have to take away Mom's sadness and be strong for her. That's too heavy a load for you to carry. That's Jesus' job, and Dad's."

Jasha blushed and shifted on the quilt.

"You've paid a big price that you shouldn't have to pay. When a boy tries to be strong for his mom, he has to put all his strength into being there for her. But you've needed us to be strong for *you*. Do you remember the times you comforted your mom when you were little?"

"Yeah," he answered, feeling a little on the spot.

"I should have been there for her, so you didn't have to. I think maybe sometimes when you felt sad you didn't tell us because you were trying to be strong for her. Am I right?"

"Yeah," he said, pursing his lips. His little chin was quivering.

"Sometimes I haven't been there to comfort your mom. But Jesus has. And I'm gonna keep on asking Him to heal my heart so I can get better at helping Him do that. When your mom feels sad, that's good that you give her a hug. But after you do, you can relax and go play; your dad will be there for her. And if I can't give her everything she needs, Jesus will be there too."

Jasha buried his face in my shoulder. I snuggled him close and spoke softly into his ear: "Whenever you're feeling sad, your mom and I are gonna ask you how you're doing. You need someone to be there for you."

Maureen knelt before each of our children and offered her own apologies. They were mostly about scaring them by raging at me for seeming to abandon her.

Unknowingly, she had also been raging at her parents for doing the same. There were times when, somewhere in the dungeon of her distant past, four-year-old Nina (Maureen's childhood nickname) was still waiting at the front window, watching anxiously up the street, bracing for the end of the world.

"Hello?" her mother would say into the phone, pretending she was speaking to the receptionist at the "bad girls' home." "Nina has been a very bad girl. You need to send the bus to take her away." She would then lay out an open suitcase. Sobbing, little Nina would pack it as well as a four-year-old knows how. Then Mom would plunk it down by the front door and order her: "Now go watch for the bus to come." The house was on a major route in Calgary, Alberta, and a bus would pass by every twenty minutes. Day after day, little Nina stood at the window, panicked at the sight of each passing bus, terrified that this might be the last time she would ever see her family.

Decades later, whenever my heart would pull away or my faulty brain would glitch, little Nina, feeling rejected, would be back at that window, crying and straining to hold back the rage she had never allowed herself to feel as a child. And in the face of her anger, little Mark would sink into the darkest corner of his past, recoiling from the violent boys at the farm and the sneering kids at school and one more loved one who couldn't understand.

… And Maureen would feel even more abandoned.

When drowning adults kick and struggle to keep their heads above the forceful undercurrents of childhood pain, they have little energy left to give the next generation what it needs. Hence, the urgency for inner healing.

Inner healing enabled Maureen to back away in baby steps from that window into the loving embrace of the mother I met a few years before she passed on. Rumor has it that when Jesus came into Audrey's life, He shut the curtains on that window, served up a hot cup of coffee, and had the first of many long chats with her about life, love, and the raising of children. His presence ignited a spark in her that flashed from her joy-filled eyes as she stepped off the plane and met newborn Michal for the first time.

As Maureen talked with the kids, I remembered Maureen's mom rocking our little Meekie, pressing her against a warm and loving heart purified by time and prayer. And I found myself thinking, "I miss you, Audrey. I wish we could have seen your jovial smile as Meekie blew out her first birthday candle. But I know we'll all join you soon enough. And we trust that you'll be waiting for us at the bus stop with Frank at your side, with that contagious smile of yours and a carton of milk and a tray of fresh-baked cookies."

I pulled myself back to the present, and Maureen and I continued our talk. We shared some of our childhood stories with the children. Not enough to make them feel responsible to comfort us. Just enough so they could understand what we meant when we told them, "The things we did that hurt you are not your fault. It was because of our brokenness."

We finished by saying, "We can't promise we'll never hurt you again, because we're not perfect; only Jesus is. But we will promise we will never hurt you on purpose. There may be times when at first we don't realize we have. But as soon as we realize it, we'll always ask you to forgive us. And if we don't realize what we've done, you can tell us, and we'll listen when you share your hurts. And we promise we'll keep on seeking healing so that we'll hurt you less and less."

The kids were now settled into the creases of the quilt like little boats anchored in a calm harbor, sheltered from a distant storm. Silently I prayed, "Lord, please make the effects of what we're doing last. And help Maureen and me grow fast enough to become grown-ups before they do." But in my heart, I knew that we needed only to persevere as best we could. Where we were lacking, Jesus would be grown-up enough.

Our children's hearts were now more open than before. But we could sense they were still holding back somewhat. For Maureen and me, the drama of that day's tears and apologies had burned with the intensity of a revival. But our children needed something more. They needed to see us continue toward what we had promised and go the distance for them. To see us stand in place as long as it would take. Arms stretched to the sides. Feet crossed. Enduring whatever was needed to restore their trust, until it was time to remove the nails and show them the emblems of our commitment ...

CHAPTER 13

The Lost Art of Restitution

I COULD SEE NO SUCH EMBLEMS on Gerald's* palms.

Nor could his children.

"Whaddya mean, they need 'restitution'? I told God I was sorry, and that was enough for Him. He forgave me. Shouldn't they do the same thing? They call themselves 'Christians'!"

In a low, soothing voice, I responded: "This isn't anything against you, Gerald. It's about your kids' hearts. They're still hurting. They need you to help them process what they feel so they can let go of the hurt."

Gerald fired back: "My question is, 'Why are they even hanging onto their hurt in the first place?' God doesn't hang onto it. He forgives and forgets!"

I paused to look for a way to get behind Gerald's stone wall. He came to see me only because his wife had persuaded him. Out in Elijah House's waiting room, she had her nose buried in a magazine—a makeshift screen behind which to wipe away tears and repair smeared makeup. She had told me, "Gerald used to be so cruel to the kids. He would say such mean things—really cutting things designed to hurt. Two months ago, he told the kids he was sorry for the first time. I'm grateful for that, and the kids are trying to be, too. But he doesn't

---

* "Gerald" is a composite of several persons.

93

understand why they can't open up and trust him yet. He thinks that by just saying, 'I'm sorry,' he can snap his fingers and make a lifetime of hurts go away."

More recently, Gerald's temper had started to leak out again; his children's hearts were shutting down again, and he didn't understand why. I had taken time to listen to his perspective and win his trust. Now I spoke carefully and with tact: "I don't think your kids are hanging on to the hurt on purpose. I think they want to let it go. But it'll be easier for them to do that if you do something to help them trust you again."

A slight, permanent snarl on Gerald's upper lip betrayed a lifetime of rage he had only recently begun to cage. It was obvious to everyone close to him that he had less of a grip on it than he thought.

"Whaddya mean, 'trust me again'? I told them I was sorry! Doesn't that prove I can be trusted? I don't need to have my nose rubbed in sins Jesus already paid for! That's behind me now. I don't need to be punished over and over again for something I've already said I'm sorry for. Jesus took all my punishment on the cross!"

"Restitution isn't punishment, Gerald. You apologized, and your kids are grateful for that. But there are lots of years of hurt built up. If they can't talk about that with you, it's like putting a cap on a volcano. When kids get to their teen years, sometimes the volcano blows up, and all that emotion becomes rebellion. I don't want you to have to go through that. And if they do try to be good and they choose not to rebel, they may do it by numbing out their feelings. And then they might be submissive to you, but they won't be able to feel connected with you. When kids share their hurts, it can feel like they're accusing you, especially if their feelings are really strong. But if you can think of it this way: when you step on someone's toes and they say, 'Ouch,' it's not an accusation. If your kids can just say, 'Ouch,' and they see that you care about that, it'll help them forgive on a deeper level. It'll help them open their hearts to you."

The upper lip curled a little higher. "Man, all this talk about feelings. When I was a kid, my parents never talked about my poor little feelings, and I turned out just fine!"

I wanted to scream, "No, you didn't!"

I bit my lip.

Gerald huffed, "Where does the Bible say that kids should talk about their feelings? I don't see that anywhere. I see a God who forgives and *forgets!*"

"Romans 12:15 says, *'Weep with those who weep.'*"

"Yeah, but they don't need to keep crying after I apologized to them. They need to stop being crybabies and accept my apology!"

"You're right that they should forgive you no matter what. Restitution can help prepare their hearts to receive the apology you already gave them. And that'll help them forgive." I reminded Gerald of the story of Zacchaeus the tax collector, a man of restitution par excellence. He did more than just say he was sorry. To heal the wounds he had inflicted, he paid back four times what he owed the people he had swindled. But I could tell that Gerald's mind was busy preparing his next defense. Before I could finish, he interrupted and snorted triumphantly, "What Zacchaeus did, happened before Jesus died on the cross. Jesus cancelled our sins, so that doesn't apply anymore. We no longer have to earn His or *anyone's* grace."

Gently, I countered, "This isn't about earning grace. Jesus' grace cancelled our sins, but not the need to heal the hearts of those we've wounded."

The wall was still up. I attempted one last tactful appeal. We ended with a moment of awkward silence. As token restitution for his blustery diatribe, Gerald offered a self-consciously vigorous handshake and a perfunctory, "Thanks for your help." He and his wife went home. The door clicked behind them. The building fell eerily silent.

I never saw Gerald again.

I turned off the lights, melted into a big, soft chair, and stared endlessly, vacantly, at tiny dust particles suspended in an amber shaft of late afternoon sun. It brightened a patch of carpet like a spotlight on an empty stage. I closed my eyes and sat motionless in the stillness of the vacant building. A cool draft from a cracked-open window gently brushed my cheek. I inhaled. I exhaled. Slowly. Deliberately. Unaware of the passing of time.

By and by, distant birdsongs began to punctuate the quiet. Life flowed slowly into the room, beckoning me back to this world. I opened my eyes and sat up, switched on a reading lamp, and thumbed through my Bible to Luke 19.

Jesus had just passed through Jericho. A throng of locals swept along on either side of Him like the wake of a slow-moving ship. In my mind's eye, I could see my imaginary Tobias who had been with John the Baptist at the Jordan River, following slightly behind and to the side of Jesus, as if surfing the crest of the wave. Near the road, not far beyond the city gate, a man of short stature was perched on a thick, sturdy tree branch, peering over the towering heads of the villagers. His despondent expression seemed to say, "I could never merit even a moment of that prophet's attention." Nevertheless, Jesus stopped, turned, and fixed His loving gaze upon him.

"Why is He taking notice of *him?*" Tobias thought, as he glanced around at other questioning faces. "This man is a tax collector. He's a thieving dog; he's as low as a Gentile's slave.[1] No self-respecting Jew would even touch him!"

But Tobias couldn't help but take note of the man's humility; instead of climbing onto a roof, Zacchaeus had chosen a tree. In his culture, no dignified man would ever climb a tree, like a child.[2] And this was a sycamore fig tree like the tree in one of Jesus' parables. During a famine, a son who had turned his back on his father spent his inheritance in riotous living. Penniless, he hired himself out to a Gentile. He fed pigs the pods that encased the figs that grew on such a tree, but the Gentile refused to let him eat pigs' food! To his Jewish neighbors back home, the boy had become lower than a Gentile; to the Gentiles he was unworthy of pigs' chow. But when this prodigal son returned home—filthy, nearly naked, and wasting away—his father lavished him with a rich robe and a signet ring (signs of authority within the family), and the seat of honor at a great banquet (Luke 15:11–27).

"Zacchaeus, come down immediately," Jesus commanded (Luke 19:5). *"I must stay at your house today."* The crowd let out a muffled gasp and fell deathly silent. The community was supposed to select the host.[3] This prophet not only had the gall to select His own host; He had shoved aside the cream of Jewish society in favor of this greedy dog! Jesus was about to cross this vermin's threshold and spend the night in his house! He would be surrounded by men of the same ilk; He would be touched by them! His feet would be washed by the servant of someone lower than a Gentile. He would make Himself unclean!

And worst of all, they would share a meal! By doing so, he would make the most solemn of covenants—a "covenant of salt." Just as salt preserves food, Jesus would agree to preserve the honor of this traitor of Israel and his despicable guests.[4] He would count Himself as their personal friend—for the rest of His life![5] A low, angry murmur rumbled along the route like a rising wave ready to smash upon the rocks. Tobias heard someone complain, "He has gone to be the guest of the worst sinner in town!"

Zacchaeus jumped down from his perch and ran toward Jesus (vs 6). The crowd divided before him, jerking away as if to avoid catching lice. Before they had a chance to turn against Jesus, Zacchaeus spoke out: *"Behold, Lord, half of my possessions I will give to the poor, and if I have defrauded anyone of anything, I will give back four times as much"* (vs 8).

"Four times?!!" Tobias thought. "Moses decreed that a man must pay back four sheep for a sheep he has stolen [Exodus 22:1]. This man is admitting he's a thief! As a chief tax collector, he has many tax collectors working under him; they all give him a cut of whatever they've earned.[6] He'll have to pay that back fourfold!" Since Jericho was one of Israel's wealthiest towns,[7] that had to be a lot of money!

After collecting taxes for the despised Roman overlords, tax collectors could demand whatever they wanted for their personal fee. Demanding high fees from families with protective young Samsons could be dangerous, but the weak were considered fair game. Tobias was astonished. "These thieves have preyed upon widows and orphans for their entire career. How is Zacchaeus going to pay all that back? He'll drive himself bankrupt!"

Tobias looked at Jesus. He saw that same expression he had seen on the face of John the Baptist—lovingkindness like he had seen in the eyes of a man who had just saved a drowning friend. Jesus bestowed upon Zacchaeus the dignity one would reserve only for a true Jew: *"Today salvation has come to this house, because he, too, is a son of Abraham"* (vs 9).

Tobias gasped. "This traitor of our people, a true Jew?" A low moan of disgust spread through the crowd, yet Tobias could read in Zacchaeus' face the message welling up in his heart: "For the first time in my life, someone believes in me and trusts in me!" The kindest, most gracious man Zacchaeus had ever encountered had just placed His own reputation on the line—not only for a tax collector, but for one He had never met! Jesus locked eyes with Zacchaeus, who lit up like a candle lit by another candle. The creases on Zacchaeus' careworn face softened and took on a glow as innocent as that of an infant being comforted. It was infused with deep, sorrowful concern for Jesus' reputation and the hearts of the countless people he had wounded.

Tobias could see Jesus' parable unfolding before his very eyes. The prodigal had come home, and his father had restored his place of honor in the community. A throng of Pharisaical older brothers stood aloof, fuming. Others stood stunned and speechless, their mouths agape. Should they forgive such a man? Should they regard him as one deserving a covenant of salt? Should they spread a banquet for him in their hearts?

Through a dark cloud of jealousy and confusion, Jesus' face shone like a bright, warm oil lamp on a cold night. To Tobias, it shone even more brilliantly than the face of John the Baptist had shone, illuminating the souls behind the faces in the crowd. Tobias could sense that silently, decisions were being made. Some pursed their lips and glared at Jesus and Zacchaeus. Others fidgeted nervously and glanced about, as if ashamed to admit that their hearts were softening. Others wept quietly—many of them widows and orphans—with kindly smiles and silent apologies for them both.

Tobias felt a tear roll down his cheek. As a former Pharisee, he had taken for granted what it meant to be a child of Abraham. For the first time in his life, he realized he had known nothing at all. But now he had a new revelation to take home to his children.

I looked up and noticed that the angle of the shaft of light had shifted. Zacchaeus' story faded from my thoughts. The white wall was tinted vermillion as the sun touched the ridge of the western hills. I snapped out of my daydream and looked at my watch; I was almost late for dinner. "I'd better go before *I'm* the one who has to make restitution to my family!" I locked up the building, ran to the car, and began the drive home along the rolling mountainsides south of the Spokane River. The lush meadows, tidy homesteads, and majestic Ponderosa pines flying past me wafted away my tensions like a balmy breeze flowing through my hair.

Many years have passed since that afternoon with Gerald. Maureen and I have moved on to establish a new ministry, Elijah Rain. I relax in my office that was once our son Jasha's second-story bedroom. He has moved on to his own position of leadership in the business world, and I'm so proud of the man he has become. I find myself wondering what became of Gerald's children. Were they able to keep their hearts open to their father? Or did they use his hard heart as an excuse to close their own hearts, even to the Father of us all? A hint of a breeze ruffles the curtains, suffusing the room with the perfume of the tall lavender lilacs outside my window. I think to myself, "What a relief it is that so few I've counseled have stiff-armed me like Gerald."

It also occurs to me that I see such fathers even less often than I once did. Over the years the shallow soil in which so many like him were planted has been gradually drying out and blowing away. It was the soil of a theology that held that all we had to do was be born again and, voila, instant perfection! Time and the hard lessons of life have cured so many of that delusion.

Not that there wasn't real truth in what Gerald believed. We truly are *"a new creation; the old things passed away; behold, new things have come"* (2 Corinthians 5:17). But the tough, long haul of discipleship has a way of reinserting the phrases our deceived internal editor has excised from the pages of Scripture. Just three verses after calling us *"new creatures"* whom Christ has *"reconciled to Himself,"* St. Paul goes on to say, *"be reconciled to God"* (vs. 20). And in Hebrews 10:14 he says, *"He **has made** perfect forever those who are **being made** holy"* (emphasis mine).

Gerald's heart didn't hold enough room for seemingly contradictory messages. "I have been made perfect forever!" he insisted, and that's all that mattered to him.

"Tell that to your kids," I thought. Gerald acquired Christ's grace at the moment he converted, but it would take a lifetime to acquire His character. His kids knew that full well. In the end, did his example tempt them to not even try to follow God? Did they explode in rebellion? Or did they numb their hearts to life and love? I have prayed that it would not be so.

Geralds of other stripes have had their own excuses to ignore the need for restitution. Unlike Protestants, the Catholics and Eastern Orthodox have always held that the Christian walk is an ongoing journey, but that truth is lost on so many whose faith is nothing but a cultural habit. Yet I know Catholic brothers and sisters who are learning that confession is about drawing close to Jesus, and that it is a primer for learning to make amends with others, especially their children. And many Orthodox are waking up to the fact that being Christian isn't about being Greek, Serbian, or Russian. It's about what their saints have always called "theosis." They are returning to their time-honored understanding of the Christian walk—it is a lifelong process of becoming like Jesus, marked by repentance, restitution, and reconciliation with God and His children.

Every strain of Christendom has marinated in its own cultural soup for far too long. But for those who thirst for God, their strenuous journey is building up potency in the only spice that can overpower the repugnant religious and cultural flavors of this age. That is, *sacrificial* love. It is a love born of intimacy with the Holy Spirit, ladled out to one child at a time by the steady hand of unwavering commitment.

As Baal's thunderhead looms and the storm encroaches, Maureen and I are encountering Garys whose trials have both softened their hearts and hardened their resolve to fulfill the work of Elijah in our time. As the waves surge, these living rocks are rising to the task. They have paid the price to turn their hearts toward their children through longsuffering repentance and the lost art of restitution that makes their repentance believable.

And Maureen and I are beginning to hear their stories …

1 Joachim Jeremias, *Jerusalem in the Time of Jesus* (Philadelphia, PA: Fortress Press, 1969), 311.
2 Kenneth Bailey, *Jesus Through Middle Eastern Eyes* (Downers Grove, IL: Intervarsity Press, 2008), 178–179.
3 Kenneth Bailey, *Jesus Through Middle Eastern Eyes*, 180.
4 James M. Freeman, A.M, *Manners and Customs of the Bible* (Plainfield, NJ: Logos International, 1972), 86.
5 Barbara M. Bowen, *Strange Scriptures that Perplex the Western Mind* (Grand Rapids, MI: Wm B. Eerdmans Publishing Company, 1944), 66.
   Fred Wight, *Manners and Customs of Bible Lands* (Chicago, IL: Moody Press 1953), 227.
6 John H. Walton, Victor H. Matthews, & Mark W. Chavalas, *The IVP Bible Background Commentary, New Testament,* (Downers Grove, IL: Intervarsity Press, 2000), 236
7 (section on Luke 17:1–2) and 240–241 (section on Luke 19:1–2).

CHAPTER 14

"To Turn the Hearts of Fathers to Their Children ..."

MANY OF THE GARYS Maureen and I have counseled have fought on the front lines so long that they have wondered aloud, "Is it really true that God will not let you be *tempted beyond what you can bear*?" (1 Corinthians 10:13 NIV). Apparently, it is. They have gone the distance and held their ground. These soldiers are returning from the battle lines to rekindle home fires with a sense of commitment forged through hardships. But they have recounted the following war stories with no degree of swagger or bravado. Their trials have divested them of the delusion that their efforts at repentance and restitution have been any more impressive than that of a toddler who hit a homerun because his daddy helped him swing the bat.

Jamison*

Before enlisting in God's army, Jamison's temper-tantrums had frightened his children into behaving like submissive little soldiers. But the soldier's training God put him through drove him to his knees before them.

---

* "Jamison" is a composite of several persons.

He enlisted a prayer counselor to help search his heart for what had compelled him to spew bitterness all over his children. Hours of confession and inner healing transformed him. "But what can I do to win back their trust?" he asked. Jamison's prayer counselor shared insights she had learned from my father at a conference in the 1970's. At that time, almost no one was preaching on the lost art of restitution (even today, hardly anyone is).

"Most people think restitution is self-punishment," my father lamented, "a penance to earn our way back into God's grace. They think it denies that Christ has paid the price for our sins. Nothing could be further from the truth! Christ has already paid that price. Restitution is the price we pay to heal hearts we have wounded. For instance, imagine borrowing your neighbor's lawnmower and breaking it. Anytime you tell God you're sorry, He forgives you. But if you tell your neighbor you're sorry and give back his broken mower expecting *him* to pay to fix it, he might not forgive you! And even if he does, he won't loan it to you again! Or if you fix it and give it back, he'll forgive you, but he might hesitate to loan it again. On the other hand, if you replace the mower with a higher quality brand and add a brand-new pair of garden shears, he won't just forgive you; he'll hope you'll borrow it again!"

My father then spoke of the sacrifice Zacchaeus made to heal the hearts of people he had defrauded. "There are many ways to make restitution," he said. "A husband can give his wife a bouquet of roses to make up for failing to listen to her heart. A father can make restitution for neglecting his children by taking them on fun outings. Or restitution can be as simple as just listening to his child talk about his hurts." He finished with these words: "What if Zacchaeus had said to the townspeople, 'God forgives and forgets, so you should too,' and then just walked away? Can you imagine how that would wound their hearts?"

Jamison felt a deep pang of conscience; surely his children's needs were more valuable than a lawn mower! He resolved to do whatever it would take to heal their hearts and restore their trust, no matter what the cost. He gouged his bank account to buy tickets to fly his entire family thousands of miles to an inner healing ministry and paid for each child to receive one-on-one counseling. He washed their feet and tearfully asked each one to forgive him. To keep his resolve never to slip back into his former ways, he flew all the way across America repeatedly for further healing. This, too, was restitution.

Josiah*

Not all parents can afford to fly their kids across the country. But to God, it's the effort, not the means, that counts. In Luke 21, a widow tithed two mites to the temple. Together, they were worth no more than the cheapest Roman coin. But that was everything she owned, so in God's eyes it was more than the wealthy ever thought of tithing.

A friend of ours felt like that widow; after a childhood of being told what a nothing he was, he found it hard to see two cents-worth in his own effort. "I earned a master's degree in counseling," said Josiah, "and when I took a class in family systems, I swore they must have used my childhood homelife as the template for an alcoholic family! I'd never realized how dysfunctional we were—the roles we played and how much damage those roles did to us all. I reacted the way children of alcoholics typically do. I sat in that class frozen to my seat, overwhelmed with shame. I doubted I'd ever be a good parent. I thought I might hurt my kids like Dad hurt me. From the time I was little, he didn't want me. He was like a little kid himself—too jealous to let Mom give me much attention. He constantly put me down. He called me 'simpleton.' He told me I'd never amount to anything;

---

*   Not his actual name.

I'd never get any favor or prosper in any way. He'd threaten and say, 'I'll beat you to within an inch of your life!' I believed it; he was frightening! He beat me with belts. Once, he even slapped me across my thighs with a shovel for taking too long to clean up the dog's mess. He came home drunk and angry twice a week. I never knew when I'd get in trouble. I could see demonic rage in his eyes—something inside him wanted to break me. When you see something like that staring out at you over and over again, it's hard to stay present. I made inner vows not to be here and not to feel the fear and pain."

"How did that affect the way you raised your kids?" I asked.

"My mind became foggy. I couldn't focus on them; it was hard to even notice them. I'd held in my anger since childhood, but it was leaking out. I thought the only way to keep from hurting them was to stay away, so I worked even longer than the fifty-five hour week my workplace required. That made me tired and more irritable. My wife would get mad at how I handled the kids. I couldn't see myself as a successful father, so I disengaged. She was a good mom, so I thought she could be the one to handle the kids. That gave me an excuse not to be involved."

"What made you realize you needed to change?"

Josiah took a moment to gather his thoughts. "I got so numb I couldn't even feel the anger. But the kids could sense it, and they thought my distance meant I was angry at them. I realized I had abdicated my place as their dad, and I could feel them pulling away. It was really hard—I had to face failure. Deep in my heart I thought, 'What's the use?' I had to fight the temptation to give up. But love compelled me; I wanted so bad to see my kids live out life well. I started going to their plays and ball games—that was the easy part of restitution. But my son was imaginative and musical, and I was athletic; I thought I wouldn't be able to connect. My daughter told me she knew I cared, but she needed me to show it with hugs; she needed to hear 'I love you' and 'I'm proud of you.' It was hard for me to start doing those things. I felt like I didn't have the authority; I hadn't earned the right. I know that sounds stupid. But I asked God to help me; I didn't want to pass on to them the lies my dad and I had grown up with: 'I deserve to be treated badly'; 'I don't deserve attention.' When I finally talked things out with my kids, I found they'd already started believing lies of their own. They thought I'd be disappointed in them if they said what they really felt. They had assumed my grouchiness was their fault."

As counselors, Maureen and I had heard stories like this countless times. When we don't talk things out with our kids, they almost always assume the worst. And sometimes we parents do too. "I had assumed that the kids might reject my overtures," said Josiah. "They didn't! When I apologized, they all forgave me! And now, they're all committed to God. They're involved in ministry. Best of all, they come to me now to talk things out!"

Josiah was understating the good outcome. Every one of his children acknowledges the changes. When they do, he blushes and wonders aloud if he truly merits their praise. But I think that in his heart, he has learned that he doesn't have to.

As a child, I felt indignant at all the Josiahs who weren't there for their children. "Why don't these dads get their act together?!" Now that I am a Josiah, I understand. There really is no act to get together. There never was. Only one man ever had His act together. For the rest of us, there is a widow's mite. Repentance multiplies it, and restitution opens our children's eyes to see the increase.

Repentance and restitution will be Baal's undoing in the coming generation. For that reason, Satan shines a glaring spotlight on the little mite in the palm of your hand, scoffs at it, and reminds you of what a "pathetic little nothing" you are. Some parents avoid the shame by denying the harm they've done. To those who step out of denial, the demons taunt: "Look at all the harm you've already done to your kids. Give up! You'll never make it up to them." And he tricks them into thinking these are their own thoughts.

But Josiah averted his gaze from that little coin's dull sheen and looked toward the gentle glow from the face of Jesus. In His eyes, Josiah could see no condemnation. When Josiah looked back at his own hand, the coin was gone, and all he could see was a nail scar.

… And he realized that this was all that his children ever really needed from him.

CHAPTER 15

"... And the Hearts of Children to Their Fathers"

NOT ALL PARENTS ARE WILLING to bear the nail scars, and some would if they could, but are just too broken to know how. But they're not the only ones responsible to stop the curse Malachi warned of (Malachi 4:5-6). He promised that God will not only *turn the hearts of fathers to their children,*" but also *"the hearts of children to their fathers."* Our parents' failure doesn't make the curse inevitable.

Layne and Shawna reminded me that when children reach out, it can change parents' lives as much as reaching out to our children changes theirs.

Layne

The powers of darkness try to deceive those who have been loved, into believing they have not. In the case of our friend Layne, they had ample help. Her mother wasted no ammunition in the pre-divorce war. "My mom used to tell me so many negative things about Dad," she said. "'Your father doesn't love us.' 'He doesn't care about his family.' 'He's stingy with his money.' 'He's mean.'"

Layne hadn't found this hard to believe. Her father's reactions to his own forgotten childhood hurts had weakened his defense against these volleys, allowing them to chase him to a distant corner of Layne's life.

... But not as distant as she had thought. Bitterness exaggerates parents' shortcomings and blinds children to the love they give. "Mom convinced me that Dad used his money as a controlling weapon, so I vowed in my heart, 'I won't put myself in debt to him.' I tore up his birthday checks; he kept sending them anyway."

"Your heart didn't know that was an expression of his love?" I asked.

"I couldn't see it that way. But God began to speak to my heart about him. When my husband and I started a small business, we realized we didn't trust our Heavenly Father to provide, any more than I had trusted my earthly father to provide. So we prayed, 'Forgive us for projecting our bitterness toward Dad onto You,' and I asked God to forgive my inner vow never to be in Dad's debt. God's favor returned, and funds began pouring in! Later, I took a class on inner healing. While the students were writing in their journals, the Holy Spirit convicted me about lies I'd believed about Dad. He was overly frugal, but he wasn't stingy; our family lived in a nice house and was well provided for. Dad wasn't a hugger, but even with a heavy class load at law school, he took time to take us kids fishing. He coached my brother's baseball team and helped us with chores and homework. I admit he was demanding; he would ask, 'Why only one A on your report card?' But he wasn't as mean as Mom made him out to be. When Mom divorced him, he stayed away from the house out of fear of criticism and the caustic things she'd say, but he still regularly drove an hour and a half to take us kids out to lunch."

I was starting to feel impressed with Layne's dad. "Sounds like he wasn't heartless. He was just broken, wanting to reach beyond his weaknesses but not knowing how."

"Yeah," Layne replied. "He was locked up, but I think he gave what he knew how to give. Through the class on inner healing, I realized I had bought into what Mom had said about Dad. I really didn't know who he was on the inside. I also learned that repenting of a root of bitterness brings freedom not only to you but to the ones you've judged."

"It frees them to be who God made them to be."

"Yes, there was so much that God had put into Dad that I hadn't seen. So I prayed, 'Forgive me for believing lies about my dad. I confess I never really knew who he was. Please show me who he truly is.' I was amazed at how quickly God answered that prayer! Just a half hour after I arrived home from class that night, he called and asked if he could come visit. I'd been married for sixteen years. During all that time, although Dad's heart was always open when we visited him, he had never taken the initiative to visit us. Mom's criticism and their bitter divorce made him afraid to reach out. And I have to confess, my resentment made it hard, too. But when I prayed what I prayed, a spiritual block lifted. My prayer set him free to show me the love he couldn't show before."

"Even though he didn't know what you had prayed?" I asked.

"Yes. And two days later he was at my door, and he gave me a big, long hug. I'd always been the one to hug him, but this time, he initiated it, and he held me really close! He'd always been shy about giving praise, but he told me, 'I was always proud of you. You're a better parent than I ever was. And if you ever wonder if you are successful in life, look at the faces of your sleeping children and see if you've succeeded beyond most parents.' Until then, Dad had called only on special occasions like Christmases and birthdays. But from that day forward, he visited often, and his new wife embraced my children as if they were her own grandchildren. Dad became my chief business advisor. This 'stingy man' even forgave a $2,000 business debt we owed him. My Mom had always said, "He doesn't care about his family,' but from then on he visited often, and he would shower us and his grandchildren with hugs and kisses."

As Layne finished her story and our call came to an end, the feeling she left me with was in stark contrast with that moment many years ago when Gerald left my office and the building fell deathly quiet, empty, and hollow. Now, the house was filled with a different kind of quiet. The Holy Spirit infused the air, pressing in on me weightlessly, like a pile of airy pillows in a snug hammock. I settled into that centered feeling you get when you've been in the presence of someone whose sojourn in life has transformed her heart into a compass of truth. And I thought to myself, "You really can open your heart to your parents even before they change."

I had known that for a long time. But when someone you know lives it out, it starts to feel like reality.

Shawna*

It especially feels real when one who lives it out has come from an abusive background. I would never have guessed Shawna had. She was one of those rare persons so close to the heart of Jesus that she overflowed with joy in spite of the fact that like Josiah, she had received hardly as much as a widow's mite of love from her adoptive mother.

"I cleaned house and made lunches while Dad brought Mom breakfast in bed," Shawna said without a hint of resentment. "I primped Mom's hair and waited on her and her natural son hand and foot, like Cinderella. I always obeyed, but I got punished nearly every day. A lot of times I didn't even know why. Mom broke sets of ping-pong paddles on me and shoved aggressive enemas into me like that traumatized girl in the movie, *Sybil.* When I was five, they discovered I was a child prodigy. I learned piano so fast that within a year, there was nothing left for my piano instructor to teach me. Onstage, I became my mother's trophy; at home, I was still her slave. After every concert

---

* Not her actual name.

she punished me for every mistake I'd made, so I never learned to like playing. I pasted on a stage-smile and kept up the charade until I graduated from high school. Then I moved out, gave up piano, and left 'Hitler's sister' to fend for herself."

As a counselor, I am amazed at the special grace God grants children like Shawna who have received less than a widow's mite of love. King David's words have proven so true: *"My father and mother have forsaken me, but the Lord will take me up"* (Psalm 27:10).

"God became the loving mother I never knew," Shawna said with awe. "He gave me the restitution Mom never gave me. He gave me a very loving husband. He led me to the best prayer counselors who could pray for inner healing. And I could always feel God's comforting presence."

"Even when your mom mistreated you?"

"Yeah," she said, "Even then. I don't know how. I just always knew He was there, comforting me. And that's what enabled me to love Mom, even when she was at her worst."

Shawna then shared a series of little miracles which I suspect were more impressive to God than raising the dead. "I chose to forgive Mom one baby step at a time, no matter what the cost. I went to stay with her for two weeks every summer. I took her put-downs because I wanted to give her the same kind of restitution I didn't receive from her when I was little—God helped me give Mom the patience and love her own mom never gave her. One summer, on the morning before I traveled to visit her, I heard the Holy Spirit say silently but very clearly, "You're not going to get along with your mother on this trip."

"As if you ever had!" I said.

"Yeah," she replied with a laugh, "but I resolved I was gonna go anyway. It really was an awful visit! Mom constantly cut me down with caustic barbs and criticisms. Nothing I did pleased her; everything I did made her angry. But I just kept praying for her and trying to love her. On my last day there, I offered to play some tapes of inspired preaching for her. Mom spat back, 'How dare you think I need to listen to this!' I felt the Holy Spirit prompting me to leave the tapes by the tape player, and I prayed for Mom all the way home. Eventually, she popped them into the player, and she even listened to them with a few old friends from the neighborhood!"

"How did your mom respond?" I asked.

"That's the best part of the story! One of her friends actually convinced her to ask Jesus into her heart! Getting past her walls had to be a miracle!"

"Did you see a lasting change in her?

"Well, I visited Mom a few months later. Before I went, Mom's friend who'd brought her to Jesus warned me on the phone, 'Your mom's still difficult, but the good news is that she's on the mend.' When I saw Mom, she was still cranky, but not as caustic as she had been. And her heart kept getting softer. When Mom got older, she had to move to a smaller apartment. I was helping her unpack boxes, and I pulled out a little red Shriner's hat. At that moment, Mom became more vulnerable than I'd ever seen her. She let me explain one of the reasons our family's emotions had been locked up for so long. When my grandfather climbed the thirty-three steps of Freemasonry, at each step he pledged allegiance to different gods—the gods of the Egyptians and Greeks and other ancient peoples."

"St. Paul called those gods 'demons,'" I noted (1 Corinthians 10:20).

"I could definitely sense they were! And I could see what they were doing to us! In the final step of Masons, Grampa honored Lucifer as the 'architect of the universe'! Mom agreed to pray to renounce our family's ties to these spirits, and it was like a dark cloud lifted off her mind. She had this moment of clarity. For the first time in her life, she asked, 'Would you please forgive me?' A few years later, she fell ill and went to be with Jesus. Her caretaker called me instead of her natural son even though he lived just a few miles away and I lived in a distant state. She knew I'd been the one who'd stayed at Mom's bedside on my long visits. I had learned how to love Mom, and her caretaker knew that."

"And you'd learned how to forgive."

"I'd learned how to forgive," Shawna repeated, nodding. "But it was hard. For years, I told God, 'I can't do this.' But I just chose to forgive anyway, again and again. When Mom was a child, she got even less love than I did, so I think she decided she didn't need it. But finally, she couldn't resist anymore. She let my love into her heart, and it was like the veil came off 'Hitler's sister.' I saw this little girl trying to be brave in a world without a mom's love. And when I saw the heart of the child she'd been, a veil started lifting off my daughter. For the first time, I could see how she must have felt when she wondered where her mommy had been all the years when I was out dating a string of Prince Charmings. I was wishing one of them would slip the glass slipper on my foot and spring me out of jail. So, I sat down with 'Cassie'*—she was all grown up by then—and I began to unpack memories with her one by one, asking her again and again, 'Would you please forgive me?'"

I paused to ponder the sacredness of that encounter. "You've really lived out the principles I'm writing about in my book," I said. "…But there's one more step in your healing I'd like you to take."

"What's that?"

"Take up your piano playing again. You gave up that gift out of resentment toward your mom. Don't let resentment own that gift; it belongs to you. Claim it back. I want to come to your concert!"

"People have been telling me that," Shawna replied, sounding a little convicted. "Your words are another confirmation." She paused a moment to contemplate that thought. "… I think I'll start playing again."

---

* Not her actual name.

But Shawna never put on that concert. Instead, a few months after my interview with her, she moved to a new home, far away. Cancer transported her to a heavenly address where she and her mom have resumed opening boxes together. Cassie remains in her earthly home where the Holy Spirit is busy digging her own daughter's boxes out of the closet, to be unpacked on another day.

I regret that I will never get to hear Shawna play. … At least not in this life. But I know that even after she buried her gift for most of a lifetime, God will grant Shawna the same grace she gave her mother who had buried her love. As I reminisce about the gift Shawna was, I can feel her joyful presence and hear that infectious giggle that punctuated our conversations. And I know that someday, by God's grace, I will hear her play piano again.

I sense a presence in the distance, in jarring contrast with Shawna's sweet spirit. In my mind's eye I picture him—a towering man with the horned head of a bull, glowing red-hot and seated on a massive throne. He is ruminating about his plans to thwart the Elijahs of our time. He taunts them: "There's more than one way to get humans to sacrifice their precious progeny! Let them become so self-absorbed that they can no longer see beyond themselves. No more milk and cookies for you, my dear little ones. Your elders will be engrossed in far more noble pursuits." He revels in the thought of making a thick, dark cloud of self-love descend upon these elders. "Yesss. Let that be their undoing," he hisses.

The man turns his horned head toward Jamison, Josiah, and Layne. He leans toward them menacingly, like a thunderhead ready to unleash its fury. But his dark cloud quickly disperses as a shining man emerges like a brilliant sunrise piercing through morning fog.

Something in the horned man's eyes betrays the fear he is hiding behind his blustery bravado. He cringes like a naughty little boy in the shadow of a looming schoolmaster, with a squeamish look you would see on the face of a schoolyard bully who has just been caught in the very act—his fist pulled back, poised for the punch.

The shining man plants His feet squarely between the bully and the three little ones. Under the weight of each step He takes, the earth nearly shakes. He reaches toward them, turns over His hands, and shows them the marks that restitution has engraved upon His palms. Restitution they never deserved but that He gave, nonetheless.

The bully swallows the lump in his throat and sulks like a child whose toys have been confiscated. Blissfully unaware of him, the three go about the business of their day. They set a carton of milk and a tray of cookies on the kitchen table and call their children in from play. The bully realizes that these three "pathetic little nothings" have all been moved well beyond his reach and that his grand plans for their "noble pursuits" are falling to the ground.

… And it begins to dawn on him that they and many more like them may soon become *his* undoing.

CHAPTER 16

They Need Us Now More Than Ever

JAMISON, JOSIAH, AND LAYNE have already become Baal's undoing. They are some of the rocks I foresaw so many years ago, towering above the waves, standing ready for those who will need to cling to them when the storm rolls in. The rising swells sway heavily against their flanks but cannot move them. Around them a vast sea of humanity drifts aimlessly, largely unaware of what's coming. Far beyond them at the distant horizon, threads of white light flash ominous warnings across a slim and narrowing band of light blue sky between dark, brooding sea and roiling, black clouds. I think to myself, "When this storm hits, will there be enough rocks to keep them all from drowning?"

Chilly gusts disrupt the balmy breeze wafting across the warm sand. The sun dims. Shadows spread quickly across the beach as the clouds roll inland. I grab the folds of my light jacket and pull them tight around me. My bare feet grow cold in the troubled surf.

I rouse myself from my waking dream, and the deafening wind dies away. Once again, I am in Post Falls, Idaho, hundreds of miles from the surging waves. I sit back and relax in our old wooden rocker by the warm fire in our little cast-iron stove. I savor the quiet, although I know that in the invisible realm, a storm truly is approaching.

To tally up the damage from the first gusts of wind, I set my laptop on a blanket pulled across my lap and pop it open to surf the web. Before I have a chance to dive into a plethora of bad news, I run across some hopeful statistics I hadn't expected. On average, fathers who live with their children are spending more time with them than fathers did in 1965![1] The trends are upward in every Western nation surveyed! In most of the same nations, mothers, too, are spending more time with their children, despite longer work hours.[2]

"Is this for real?" I ask. "This sounds too good to be true!" It does seem true at least for the young Christian parents Maureen and I know. We see a deeper concern and fervor in them than in previous generations, especially the fathers.

"Still," I think to myself, "something isn't making sense. If these parents are spending more time with their kids, why aren't we seeing more well-adjusted children? And why are so many kids still feeling neglected?" I read on and find that parents may be too stressed out to turn that extra time into quality time. Over a recent eight-year period, depression among young adults rose sixty-three percent. Serious psychological stress rose seventy-one percent. Suicidal thoughts and outcomes rose forty-seven percent.[3] And the men are doing worse than the women. So, I well understand why sixty-three percent of fathers say that being a good dad is harder than it was in past generations.[4]

I read that working moms have the added stress of having to cut back time with husbands, friends, relatives, and civic activities to devote more time to both career and children.[5] Feeling unsupported, many are anxious, worn out, and sleep deprived. This is making time with their children more tense, and stressed-out kids are acting out through bad behavior and lower grades in school.[6]

It's hard to be present for your kids when you're drowning in your own troubles. Nowadays, young adults Maureen and I counsel so often say to us, "Yes, my parents spent time with me, but it felt like they were present in body only."

Through my joust with the spider, I learned where a lot of parents' inner struggles come from. To numb the pain of living in a hurtful world, I vowed in my heart to disconnect in so many ways. By the time I grew up and had children of my own, my subconscious inner vows ("I won't feel," "I won't need," "I won't show my heart to anyone") were waging a tug-of-war with me that sapped my strength. Although I desperately wanted to be present for my kids, these inner vows yanked the rope in the opposite direction. Childhood bitterness leaked to the surface like gas from a ruptured pipeline, sending up toxins that dragged me into depression and clouded my thoughts. I spent much of what strength I had left on trying to find my way through the fog, leaving little energy for my children. Despite my best efforts be present, I often neglected them even while spending time with them. And when I beat myself up for that, shame focused me inward and made me even more self-absorbed.

My struggle was only one variation on a theme that, as prayer counselors, Maureen and I have seen in countless lives. And as if all that weren't enough, young parents are trying to stay committed to their children in a culture that showers them with more family-destroying temptations than in any generation before them. It replaces eternal truths with whatever feels right at the moment. Commitment to unchanging moral laws feels fine until your beliefs are ridiculed. Vowing lifelong commitment to your mate feels exhilarating when you slip the ring on, but not when you're arguing about how to salvage your happiness. When you're tired, playing a game with your child is a lot less appealing than watching TV with him. Our culture endorses Baal's plan for a life of moral ease and urges us to compromise whenever commitment stops feeling good. Once the domino of moral law begins to fall, the rest of the dominos must eventually fall—commitment to faith, to church, to marriage, and finally, commitment to children.

My heart goes out to parents who are trying keep the last domino from falling. Since 1960, the number of our nation's children living without their biological father has gone from one in twelve[7] to one in three[8]—a fourfold increase. And more than one in four live with no father at all.[9] The U.S. is the most fatherless nation in the Western world, and other nations are following close behind. Numbers magnify the chaos approaching from that gloomy horizon. Fatherless kids are twenty times more likely to have behavioral disorders, ten times more likely to end up in a chemical abuse center, five times more likely to commit suicide, thirty-two times more likely to run away from home, fourteen times more likely to commit rape, and twenty times more likely to go to prison![10]

For many years, Maureen worked in local schools helping troubled kids with their schoolwork. Every year, there were more fatherless children, and every year their behavior was worse than before. She wondered how many of them would end up in prison.

Moms, more than dads, are holding their ground; only one in twenty-five kids are living with a dad but not a mom. The same number have neither a dad nor a mom, raising the motherless rate to about one in twelve.[11] I breathe a sigh of relief, until I read that this is also a four-fold increase since 1960.[12] Mothers are now in the same place fathers were at that time; if this trend remains unchecked, mothers will go the way of fathers. For the first time, young men Maureen and I counsel are telling us their wives have abandoned them and their children. Without a mother to focus them, children are more prone toward being hyperactive and delinquent.[13] Without her comforting embrace, they are lonelier and more isolated, unable to bond, fearful, moody, clingy, dependent, demanding, and unmotivated.[14] To survive the storm ahead, children will need that which enabled King David to survive his own personal storm. He cried out to God about enemies who were like *"Roaring lions [that] open their mouths wide against me"* (Psalm 22:13 NIV). But he found peace in this: *"You made me trust in You, even at my mother's breast"* (vs. 9 NIV).

Father Seraphim Rose, an Orthodox leader who passed on in 1982, prophesied, "The psychological trials of dwellers in the last times will be equal to the physical trials of the martyrs." This prophecy is coming true! His words cast light on the admonition I gave at that leaders' conference years ago—that if they wanted revival to come soon, they must make their children their priority. I now realize that God wasn't scolding them; He was sympathizing with them. He knew their trials. He understood how tempting it could be to use ministry to distract themselves from the mounting stress at home. He wouldn't give them more reason to do so by sending throngs of new converts too soon for them to disciple. Nor would He do that to their followers. God wanted revival to be part of the cure for the stress families were facing, not its cause.

I sense that the Holy Spirit was and is saying something like this to parents: "For now, just stay focused on Me. Keep turning to Me in repentance until repentance becomes a lifestyle. You will discover that every prayer of repentance allows a little more of My love into your heart, healing and enlarging it until sacrificial love and commitment become second nature. Then there will be room in your heart for both your children and all the others I plan to send your way."

I can vouch for that message because for me, that lifestyle has made the spider lose the battle.

In short, the Holy Spirit is saying: "When enough Christians are living a lifestyle of repentance, it will be time for revival."

As I consider sharing this message, I anticipate the inevitable questions people will ask. "How many Christians are 'enough'

Christians?" And, "How do we know when it will be time?" So here's the answer: we don't, for if we knew, we might make that our focus. The Father wants us to prepare for that day by drawing closer to His loving heart and to the hearts of our children.

One day, while contemplating how my generation might help the next generation prepare for that day, I happened upon an article in *The Atlantic* magazine titled, "The Nuclear Family Was a Mistake."[15] My blood boiled. "More of this anti-family garbage!" I fumed. "This writer is attacking the one thing we need the most!"

Then I realized he wasn't.

He meant only that the nuclear family *by itself* was a mistake. Until 1850, he said, families lived in clans, with close relatives either in the home or nearby. If parents were neglectful or they divorced or died, grandparents, aunts, uncles, and in-laws were rocks whom children could cling to through the storms of life. Then, in the late 1800's and early 1900's, young parents left their clans and migrated to the cities for factory jobs. Loneliness drove young men to marry three and a half years earlier than they had in 1890, and young women married more than two years earlier. Younger, less mature couples were left to handle the stress of parenting with far less help than before.

For a short time, it worked. In the 1950's and 60's, mothers stayed home with their kids, and fathers could easily finance that; by 1961, men in their late twenties earned four times what their fathers had earned. And without air conditioning and a large selection of TV channels, neighbors lived on each other's front porches and chatted over backyard fences. Kids played kickball in each other's front yards. Nuclear families up and down the block banded together, forming what amounted to makeshift clans. They watched out for each other. If you were ill, your neighbor would volunteer to shovel the snow off your sidewalk. If you ran low on flour, you could borrow a cup next door. If your kid did something naughty away from home, other parents would lovingly correct him for you.

Then came trouble in paradise. Men's wages no longer kept up with the cost of living; moms could no longer afford to stay home. It was good that mothers were freer to work; it was bad that they had to. Motherhood was devalued. It became legal to kill your own unborn child. Neighborhood clans dissolved. Air-conditioning and TV drew people from the porch into the living room. Video games and online pornography drew them from the living room into the back room. We no longer knew our next-door neighbors by name. Grandparents retired to warmer climates. The family had already been quietly undermined by an expanding divorce rate. From 1870 to 1920, divorce increased fifteen-fold and continued to increase more slowly for several decades, yet still remained low. Then, in the 1960's and 70's, it exploded.[16] As family life eroded, young people imploded.

Yes, the nuclear family—*all by itself*—was a mistake.

As family life eroded, so did society. My parents could take for granted a culture that supported the values they raised their kids by. Nearly everyone revered the Ten Commandments; even atheists followed them (except, of course, the ones about God and the Sabbath). We didn't have to put a lock on our door until I was eleven years old. Those of us who lived in smaller towns could leave for a two-week vacation with nary a worry that anything would be missing when we returned. I remember the day in 1966 when my dad installed the first lock on our front door.

"Why do we need to do that?" I asked incredulously.

"People aren't as honest as they used to be," he sighed. "*Thou shalt not steal* doesn't mean what it used to mean. People up and down the street are having locks put on."

At that moment I sensed a shifting wind in the world outside our door, and for the first time, I felt foreboding about the direction our world was headed.

125

I fold my laptop and imagine cracking open the door to take another peek at that turbulent horizon. I see an anchor—the Judeo-Christian ethic that once tethered us to moral sanity—being hoisted out of the deep. It is being replaced with something that looks nothing like an anchor—the postmodern precept that *feelings* define reality. "If it *feels* good, do it!" was my generation's tagline. Feelings became the diviner of truth; it became popular to say, "You have your truths and I have mine." We concocted any "truths" that made us feel good. Without shared truths, there was nothing left to restrain selfishness; each person's own feelings came first. We became self-absorbed, and the stress of living in such a chaotic world made us even more self-absorbed.

Now our children indulge the feelings we weren't there to listen to; they have taken our foolishness and are running with it. Inevitably, one person's feelings must clash with another's. If you believe in absolutes, people who don't feel good about that accuse you of being "intolerant" while insisting that your belief must not be tolerated. If you disagree about a moral issue—no matter how lovingly or respectfully—you are called a "hater." And it may get worse for our grandchildren.

They need us now more than ever.

What, then, can my generation do to come alongside young parents? By portraying the Father's loving heart to them as mothers and fathers in Christ. We can start by letting go of a defeatist attitude and recognize that no matter how worn down the struggles have made us feel, God has given us the strength to do it. During the same eight years when depression and psychological stress rose so rapidly among young adults, there was no increase at all among those of us over sixty-five.[17]

How can we invest that strength? First, by rediscovering the "parent" in "grandparent." Grandparents used to understand that the most important task of their sunset years was investing time and love in their grandchildren. Nowadays, we're moving in droves to climates where we can devote our remaining years to basking in the sunshine and improving our golf-swing. Only once in my lifetime have I heard a sermon urging us to reverse this trend and stay near our families at a time when they need us the most.

And we can rediscover the concept of the "godparent." For centuries, all churches required parents of every newborn to enlist godparents to help them raise their child, and every adult convert was taken under a godparent's wing before joining the Church. These mother and father figures visited with them, had them over for dinner, mentored them, walked them through crises, and prayed for them as they would their own children. Orthodox Christians still practice this lifelong commitment. Some other denominations still do, but for many, including the one in which I was raised, it is a fading formality. I don't remember ever meeting my godparents; I don't even know who they were. (Today, Maureen and I have new godparents.) Nowadays, a lot of Christians have never even heard of the concept of a godparent. I have almost never heard anyone advocate that churches should resume this practice.

We can also remind ourselves that the church is supposed to be an extended family. It used to be that. Not anymore. Not in an age when we divorce our church family and go looking for another one every time the pastor won't do what we want, the sermons aren't fascinating enough, or the Sunday morning concert doesn't sound professional enough. Meanwhile, we think we can cure our nation's ills by touting our politics and seeking signs and wonders.

Maureen and I pray that valiant young fathers and mothers don't give up the fight. We pray that when the coming storm hits full force, they and their children will find the rocks they can cling to. We pray that we all take our tasks as grandparents and godparents more seriously. And we pray that our generation accepts the calling that will make us ready for these tasks …

1   "The Importance of Dads in an Increasingly Fatherless America," *The Heritage Foundation*, Accessed August 6, 2020, https://www.heritage.org/marriage-and-family/commentary/the importance-dads-increasingly-fatherless-america.
2   Esteban Ortiz-Ospina, "Are Parents Spending Less Time With Their Kids?", *Our World in Data* (December 14, 2020), Accessed October 30, 2021, https://ourworldindata.org/parents-time-with-kids.
3   "Mental health issues increased significantly in young adults over last decade," *ScienceDaily* (March 15, 2019), Accessed September 1, 2020, https://www.sciencedaily.com/releases/2019/03/190315110908.htm.
    "Mental Health by the Numbers," NAMI (National Alliance on Mental Illness), Accessed September 1, 2020, https://www.nami.org/mhstats.
4   Gretchen Livingston and Kim Parker, "A Tale of Two Fathers, More are Active, But More Are Absent," *Pew Research Center, Social and Demographic Trends*, Accessed September 4, 2020, https://www.pewsocialtrends.org/2011/06/15/a-tale-of-two-fathers/.
5   D'Vera Cohn, "Do Parents Spend Enough Time With Their children?" (January 17, 2007), *PRB*, Accessed November 1, 2021, https://www.prb.org/resources/do-parents-spend-enough-time-with-their-children/.
6   Brigid Schulte, "Making Time for Kids? Study Says Quality Trumps Quality," *The Washington Post* (March 28, 2015), Accessed November 1, 2021, https://www.washingtonpost.com/local/making-time-for-kids-study-says-quality-trumps-quantity/2015/03/28/10813192-d378-11e4-8fce-3941fc548f1c_story.html.
7   "The Majority of Children Live With Two parents, Census Bureau Reports," *The United States Census Bureau*, November 17, 2016, Accessed August 31, 2020, https://www.census.gov/newsroom/press-releases/2016/cb16192.html.
8   "More Data on the Extent of Fatherlessness," *Fathers.com*, Accessed August 31, 2020, https://fathers.com/statistics-and-research/the-extent-of-fatherlessness/.
9   Posted by Christopher A. Brown, "What's the Status of Father Absence Ahead of the Twenty Twenty Census?", *The Father Factor*, Accessed September 3, 2020, https://www.fatherhood.org/fatherhood/father-absence-ahead-of-the-2020-census.
10 "Statistics," *The Fatherless Generation*, Accessed August 6, 2020, https://thefatherlessgeneration.wordpress. com/statistics/
11 "More Children Live with Just Their Fathers than a Decade Ago," *Census Bureau* (November 16, 2017), Accessed August 28, 2020, https://www.census.gov/newsroom/press-releases/2017/living-arrangements.html.
12 "More Children Live with Just Their Fathers than a Decade Ago."
13 "Child Behavior Problems With an Absent Mother," *Modern Mom*, Accessed August 28, 2020, https://www.modernmom.com/79653770-3b45-11e3-8407-bc764e04a41e.html.
14 "How an Absent Mother Affects Children," *You Are Mom*, Accessed August 28, 2020, https://youaremom.com/children/absent-mother-affects-children/.
15 David Brooks, "The Nuclear Family Was a Mistake," *The Atlantic* (March 2020), Accessed April 5, 2021, theatlantic.com/magazine/archive/2020/03/the-nuclear-family-was-a-mistake/605536/.
16 Brooks, "The Nuclear Family Was a Mistake."
17 "Mental health issues increased significantly in young adults over last decade."

CHAPTER 17

A Calling
We May Not Want to Hear

WHETHER BELIEVERS OF MY GENERATION become rocks for the next generation depends on what calling we answer. I take out my phone and scroll through social media. People are drowning, and God's people are trying to pull them out of the soup by posting the latest prophetic word promising imminent revival. They urge us to pave the way for it by championing political causes: "Elect righteous candidates!" "Restore the ideals of our founding fathers!" Such causes are quite worthy of promotion (when thoughtfully considered and graciously expressed), but how many are posting a call to turn the hearts of fathers to their children? It's hard to go there when all the hullabaloo is about being on the winning political or cultural team. Repenting to our children isn't as exciting as all that.

I slip my phone back into my pocket, reel in my overactive thinker, and focus for a while on just being with God. As I quiet my mind, a "random" memory pops up, and I recognize the stamp of the Holy Spirit upon it. A seminary professor shared with our class about his ministry trip to Calcutta, India. Although he and his Baptist coworkers felt some disdain toward the Catholic Church, nonetheless they paid an unscheduled visit to a servant of the faith revered by Christians of all stripes: Mother Teresa.

They were surprised that even with so many nuns to do her bidding, she herself answered the door! She had been sweeping the entryway of the convent, taking her turn with the other nuns at simple acts of service. From under her signature blue and white head-covering, she greeted her visitors with her innocent and radiant smile. She disappeared into a back room and reemerged with a platter laden with fresh cups of tea. Then, shyly and sweetly but with authority, she raised a bony finger and admonished them, "Do not come here because you want to help the poor people." Her visitors sat puzzled and slightly stunned. She continued: "There are too many poor people here. If you come here for their sake, you will drown in them. Come here because you love Jesus."

The missionaries relaxed. Mother Theresa was not minimizing the poor; she was just redirecting the missionaries' focus off of ministry and onto the One for whom they minister. Her love for Jesus was so palpable that they came away feeling *His* love for the poor, which had transformed hers into an inexhaustible cup. And they learned from her that it was not their job to turn the whole world around; it was their job to simply be fathers and mothers to the few whom God would send their way.

And that, paradoxically, is what will turn the world around.

My thoughts turn to the many Christians I've met who thought they were going to turn the world around. Proudly, they announced: "A prophet told me I will have a worldwide ministry!" After hearing this countless times, I began to question how such a huge number of people could possibly be gifted with a worldwide ministry. Nowadays, I don't hear these prophecies nearly as often. I suspect that's because many of them never came true. And maybe the few for whom they did come true have discovered that fame and influence are not an inexhaustible cup. They simply can't satisfy the soul.

That's all for the better, for I sense that to keep from going under, there's something far more important that the next generation will need from us. They'll need us to answer a calling we may not want to hear—one we would never expect to fulfill all those grandiose prophecies (although it may very well). It is the calling to become an elder. No, I don't mean "Elder" as an official church title. I mean an older person who has been transformed by the trials of life into a wise and loving spiritual father or mother.

Nowadays, everyone wants to be a rock star or millionaire by age thirty. But in Bible times, every young man's dream was to become a *zaken* (Hebrew for "elder")—a white-bearded sage under a shady tree, surrounded by youths seated in rapt attention, eagerly drinking in the wisdom he had accumulated over a lifetime. Until several years ago, I didn't sense much hunger for this among the youth. But not long ago, my older brother Loren (who recently passed into the arms of Jesus) who had a keen ear for the Holy Spirit, told me he sensed that many young hearts were beginning to soften toward their elders. Young men and women were yearning for this kind of stable refuge, and more than that, a spiritual mother or father—a rock to cling to in the coming chaos. "A window of opportunity has opened," he told me. "I sense that we must walk through it soon or it will close. If it closes, it won't open again for several decades, and our generation will miss out on a great move of God."

I fondly reminisce about where my friends and I found such refuge when I was young—in the "neighborhood Gramma." Back then, every small town and city neighborhood had one. While we chowed down on treats hot from her oven, dear old Mary Mott would utter the simplest truths, like "Jesus loves you" and "God has a plan for your life." From anyone else's mouth, these would sound like clichés. But in her, the trials of life and the commitment of faith had distilled them into profound wisdom. The messenger had become the message. Today, when I ask young audiences how many of them have a neighborhood Gramma, few raise their hands, and sometimes none at all. A lot of them are clueless about what I'm even talking about.

Our dear old friend Rose Marie Borelli (who recently passed on to heaven) was one. She taught a lot of us what fame and influence are really about. She founded a center for Inner Healing in the Chicago suburbs, called Freedom House. Persons have gone there for help from all over the Midwest and beyond. But that pedigree isn't what we remember the most about her. We cherish the memory of Rose Marie more as a neighborhood Gramma. Before going into ministry full time, she would rise every morning at 3:30 to catch two buses to work. When she returned home in the late afternoon, the neighborhood kids would always be waiting to carry her groceries and packages into the house. There, they would find candy and treats and most importantly, love, of which many received so little at home. Every Monday, she would welcome them in for Bible study. She persuaded many of them to ask Jesus into their hearts, and she counseled many of them for free.

Her daughter, Mari Anne, remembers most fondly a little African American boy named Angel whom Rose Marie introduced to Jesus, and soon thereafter, his brothers, sisters, and many adult relatives. The entire extended family called her "the Angel Lady" and phoned her for wisdom about the Bible, heaven, and Jesus. "Children" of every age and race trusted her to be Gramma.

A number of years ago, Rose Marie counseled Maureen and me. (Counselors need counseling too!) As good as the counseling was, what I remember most is her love. She called me "sweetie." No other professional counselor could get away with that, but, coming from her mouth, there was nothing unprofessional about it. To transform a heart, Rose Marie didn't need to sound professional; she just needed to sound like Rose Marie. Nor did she need to be influential or important. She just needed to share the love of Jesus.

I think that in heaven, that's what Rose Marie is famous for. I once read about a woman like her in a C.S. Lewis novel, *The Great Divorce*. In the book, a group from hell takes a bus trip to heaven to decide whether they would like to surrender their souls to God and choose to live there. (Most of them choose to return to hell, but that's another story.) One of them encounters a glorious woman heralded by a parade of angelic beings, musicians, children she had loved while on earth, and even animals that had come under her gentle touch. The visitor from hell guesses that this is a woman who had been famous in his lifetime. His guide answers that she was not; she was just a neighborhood mom who loved everyone as if they were her own sons and daughters. "Ye have heard," says the guide, "that fame in this country and fame on earth are two quite different things."[1]

With that in mind, I suspect that many may very well attain their prophesied world-changing ministry. But I doubt it will often bring fame in this world. They may not establish a ministry or preach at a podium, but neither did the father of our faith, Abraham. He, too, received a prophecy that he would change the world: *"I will make you into a great nation … and in you all the families of the earth will be blessed"* (Genesis 12:2–3). In his lifetime, all he saw of this is what happened in his own little household. He had a child in his old age, and he was faithful to love him. That son, Isaac, didn't see the promise fulfilled either; he merely raised two sons in the faith—Esau and Jacob. Nor did Jacob see the promise fulfilled. Although he blessed his twelve sons with promises of future greatness (Genesis 49), they, too, never saw this fulfilled in their lifetimes. But out of them came twelve tribes who gave us our Bible and our Messiah, and thus, our very reason for living. Today, the descendants of Jacob (whom God renamed "Israel") are the most gifted and prosperous people group on earth.

Will we be satisfied with this kind of "worldwide" ministry? Some may achieve a degree of fame like Rose Marie, founding influential ministries like hers. But what will make their ministries effective will be that they have learned how to love at their own kitchen tables. And if, like Rose Marie, their hearts have been tempered by the trials God has put them through, any fame and acclaim they do attain won't matter to them anyway.

I sense there is another reason why our calling is one we might not want to hear. That is, that more of the next generation than ours will rise into prominent positions of influence. I have long sensed that a remnant of the generation whose catchphrase was "Never trust anyone over thirty," will do its greatest ministry in old age—like Caleb who at eighty-five led Israel's next generation into the Promised Land (Joshua 14:10). How fitting that will be. The "worldwide" ministry many of my generation will carry on will be to love and heal the lost and wounded youth of the next generation and launch some of them into world-changing prominence while we stand back in the shadows, unknown and uncelebrated.

Like Abraham, Isaac, and Jacob, our world-changing effect may not be felt for generations. Unlike them, we may be entirely forgotten. As disconcerting as that may sound, the struggles and repentance that soften our hearts should keep us from becoming jealous of our children and grandchildren. For like Mother Teresa, Mary Mott, and Rose Marie, all that will matter to us will be …

… that we loved them.

---

1   C.S. Lewis, The Great Divorce (New York, NY: Collier Books, MacMillan Publishing Co., 1946), 107.

CHAPTER 18

What Will Change the World the Most?

IN MY YOUTH, I HAD THE PLEASURE of being loved and mentored by many Mary Motts and Rose Maries. Most friends my age savor memories like these. But I recall very few from from my generation who found the same kind of mentoring from a wise male elder. At that time, faith was largely considered a woman's concern. Women's faith empowered them to become spiritual mothers, first to their children and then to others God sent their way. Our fathers showed us how to change the oil in the car, but not many could show us how to plumb the meaning of life. If only they had known the power God invests in the spiritual head of a household! A survey revealed that if a child is the first in the family to accept Christ, there is a 3.7 percent chance the rest of the family will follow. If Mom is the first, the chance is 17 percent. But if Dad is the first, it is 93 percent![1] What will change the world the most? The answer is obvious.

FATHERS.

But will our children's conversion withstand the pressures of a compromised culture as they watch their parents falter under a load of emotional stress? I look at other online statistics: around 40 percent of pastors' kids have had a season of serious doubts about their faith, and 33 percent have left the church. These figures are nearly the same for children of Christians not in professional ministry. Still, there is hope; only 7 percent no longer call themselves followers of Christ. In the midst of their doubts, the 93 percent still cling to some semblance of faith.[2] But will it be enough to enable prodigals to find their way back home?

Again, why has God taken us older ones through so many trials? To build into our character the kind of commitment that will keep us waiting and watching until the prodigals return. In gratitude for the women who have held their ground all these years, it is time that we men join them and in so doing, pay them this restitution.

A man doesn't have to be a biological father to do that. Jesus had no biological sons, but He did have twelve spiritual sons. At age fifty-seven, my friend Ben* has likewise never married, yet he has been a spiritual father to fifteen young men. He has discipled them through bible study and prayer, shared meals and the joys of life, and walked many of them out of pornography addictions. He has gone toe-to-toe with them, calling out selfishness for what it is, yet they have come away feeling affirmed instead of chastised. Even young men with loving fathers at home send him Father's Day cards. Remarkably, this older bachelor has been able to successfully coach his young disciples regarding relationships with women. So far, nine have tied the knot, and they are *all* happy in their marriages. Ben is preparing the other six for the possibility of future marriage.

As a teenager, Ben saw godly spiritual parenting modeled through a couple with whom he spent nearly every weekend. His parents loved him, but no parents—no matter how loving—are sufficient for every need. Ben attended church and youth group weekly while staying overnight at this couple's house. He watched them lead a life of continual repentance that built into them the gracious, unconditional love and forgiveness Jesus modeled to His disciples. They also showed

---

* Not his actual name

him that conflict isn't always evil; it can be a tough but loving call to turn hearts back to God's ways.

Ben has dedicated his life to passing this couple's wisdom on to the next generation, laying down his life for anyone the Holy Spirit sends his way. He sent me the following story of a young man he took under his wing:

Mike* was a red-headed, freckle-faced little boy who bounded into my first-grade classroom over thirty years ago. He was excited to be in school and was glad that he got a guy for his teacher.

He was a curious, artistic little guy. He loved to cook. He was always baking with his mom and brought me homemade chocolate chip cookies every chance he got. He had a real gift; they were really good! Mike was always clowning around. He also loved to sing and dance. He loved singing along with the radio and loved music class. He was always showing me the latest dance moves. He was a gymnast and a fantastic swimmer.

Mike and I became pretty good pals. After he finished first grade, he was in my kid's choir in church, and I was fortunate to be his children's pastor. He loved the Lord and was active in church; I had the honor of baptizing him when he was thirteen. We kept in touch. I was grateful to be able to spend birthdays and Christmases with him and his family for a number of years.

Mike came from a very rich family; his dad was the president of a bank. He worked long hours and traveled a great deal. He always made sure Mike had every material thing he needed. Mike's mother was an interior designer who worked part time so she could be there for her only child. She would often tell me she was thankful for the

---

* Not his actual name

time I spent with Mike, because his father always worked late and never had time for him. She was thankful that I was a wholesome role model for him.

When Mike went off to college, we would often write back and forth. I was proud to attend his graduation. He graduated with a degree in interior design. His degree would take him to New York.

Three years ago, I had the opportunity to visit New York for the very first time. While there, Mike and I had dinner and watched *Spiderman*. It was amazing! After the show, Mike said he needed to tell me something. I could see by the serious look on his face that this was going to be heavy. He told me he was so thankful that he could see me in New York. He thanked me for always being there for him and for never judging him. He told me he appreciated my love and devotion to a Christianity that was genuine. He told me that he tried to do the same thing, but he just couldn't. He knew that Jesus loved him, but he didn't know how to stop this behavior he knew was not right. He told me he had been with a number of men intimately, and he felt empty. Then he told me that he had AIDS and was afraid of dying. He was afraid that he was going to be alone. He told me he had intended to commit suicide, but then I called and told him I was coming to New York and wanted to see him.

I told Mike I loved him and that when the time came, I would be there for him. I reached out and gave him a big bear hug, and we cried together. I can still hear him saying to me that he was shocked that, unlike his family, I wasn't afraid to touch him. He prayed with me to return to his childhood faith. From then until his death, he never again engaged in homosexual activities.

The next week, Mike finally got up enough courage to tell his mom and dad what he had struggled with. His father called him a "family disgrace" and told him he was no longer his son and would burn in hell. He told him this would probably kill his mother since she had stage-four lymphoma and had been struggling. But Mike's mother told him she loved him and always would. She passed away four months later. I was asked to sing at her funeral. Mike's dad barely acknowledged his son's grief; he didn't know how to handle emotions.

Mike moved to be near me about a year ago. He became very ill, and I would often visit him in the hospital. The doctors and nurses thought I was his father. Mike's battle with AIDS was rough to watch. His father refused to see him (although he did pay for his medical bills).

One night I was awakened by a call from the hospital informing me that Mike's passing was imminent. I immediately went to his room and found a frail, frightened young man, shaking. I gently went to his bed and took his hand, and he squeezed it. I told him I was there, and that I would stay with him as long as he needed me. I sang "Jesus loves me" and a chorus of "I will always love you" as I held him in my arms. At about 1:30 in the morning, Mike took his last breath.

Today, my heart aches because Mike isn't here, and his father never gave Mike the chance to say goodbye to him. When Mike passed away, I called his father and told him Mike was no longer with us. He paused and asked if I could take care of everything. He would pay for the memorial service but couldn't be there because an urgent trip was going to require all his attention. The last thing he said to me was that he was sorry he wasn't more like me. He wanted to be but just couldn't. He thanked me for being more of a father to his son than he ever could. He told me I was a genuine Christian and asked if we could stay in touch. I said, "Of course."

Later, he called and invited me to dinner. At dinner, he asked me why Jesus is so important to me. He asked, "Is it too late for me?" I led him in the Sinner's Prayer. He began to cry. He asked God to forgive him for neglecting his son and asked me to give him pictures I had taken of Mike. He carries his son's picture in his wallet wherever he goes.

After that, I became a father to him, too.

Ben is a testament to the truth that a heart that has been tempered with love is a heart that can be a father (or "neighborhood Grampa") to anyone.

I wish I could be a father to everyone. But I picture the millions without fathers and the millions more whose fathers are fathers in name only, and I remember the words of Mother Teresa: "Don't come here because you want to help the poor people. Come here because you love Jesus." For one last time, I imagine gazing at that endless sea of humanity and the dark waves beyond them. I choose to trust that the Lord has them all in His big strong arms and that somehow, with or without the help of an earthly father, He will come through for everyone who seeks Him. And I remind myself of the words of David in Psalm 27:10 NIV: *"Though my father and mother forsake me, the Lord will receive me."*

I hand the children of the world over to God's care and turn my gaze away from the gathering storm and into the gentle face of Jesus. The winds subside as I walk from one world into another, back into the quiet joy of our little kitchen. Maureen spreads wide our white lace curtains to let in more of the morning sun. I fetch a pitcher of milk from the fridge and place a few glasses around the table. She spreads out a batch of cookies on a floral-patterned china platter next to a vase of fresh-picked daisies. Together, we walk back to the door, open it wide, and wait for the ones He will send our way …

1   Steve Wood, "Why the New Evangelization Needs a Focus on Fathers," Dads.org (February 22, 2016), Accessed September 4, 2020, https://dads.org/fatherhood/why-the-new-evangelization-needs-a-focus-on-fathers/.
2   "Prodigal Pastors' Kids: Fact or Fiction?", Barna (November 11, 2013), Accessed September 4, 2020, https://www.barna.com/research/prodigal-pastor-kids-fact-or-fiction/.

CHAPTER 19

The Foundation for Revival

As Maureen and I hold the door for the wayfarers finding their way to the revival in our little kitchen, I can't help but hope we won't miss out on the next revival God has planned for the world beyond our front door. "What will the coming revival look like?" I muse. My friends all expect a repeat of our nations' past revivals—it will start off with a bang heard round the world and spread like wildfire to stadiums and auditoriums across the land. In short order, multitudes of new converts will transform society in ways the world has never seen. "Is that what we can expect?" I ask. "And if so, how can we make it last?"

A few years ago, these questions drew me to a nearby Christian university library. I plunked myself down on a padded wooden chair in a secluded corner and scooted noisily across the linoleum into a study cubicle. As I sat in the dead silence of the endless rows of bookshelves, I wondered how involved the Sandfords might have been in past revivals. I closed my eyes, relaxed, and imagined sailing with them into the new world on a balmy summer day in 1638. The relentless ocean breeze died down as their creaking wooden vessel glided from the rolling sea into the lightly ruffled waters at the mouth of the Charles River. The silence of primeval forests along the shorelines was broken only by the song that the rigging hummed and the gentle slicing of the waters at the bow. Soon, faint shouts of recognition could be heard across the quiet expanse upstream as the ship neared the growing hamlet of Cambridge in the British colony of Massachusetts.

The gangplank was lowered, and the Sandfords disembarked. As their feet touched new soil for the first time, their hearts overflowed with dreams of a land where they could live out their faith without fear of government oppression. They would not be disappointed; America would enjoy not only religious freedom, but more revivals than most nations! And although the fires of revival would die out again and again, each time, by God's undeserved grace, our nation would be brought back to faith and granted another chance at moral sanity.

I drew myself back to the present and began pulling books off the shelf. I read that, on the eve of the First Great Awakening of the 1730's and 40's, it was a rare believer who still knew what those early Sandfords had known—that faith is a real relationship with God.[1] A lot of people had chosen the philosophies of the Enlightenment over the dry religion of the age, and some had become atheists. The evangelist, George Whitefield, warned: "The Christian world is in a deep sleep. Nothing but a loud voice can wake them out of it."[2]

A loud voice did awaken them. During the First Great Awakening, people rediscovered the God they had forgotten, and church attendance skyrocketed. Although few white Christians condemned slavery (the evangelists George Whitefield and Jonathan Edwards actually owned slaves),[3] revivalists preached that persons of all races were created equal. So, for the first time, a number of white churches welcomed slaves who converted in large numbers. Some became deacons, and a few became pastors.[4]

In one sense, the call of Elijah (prophesied in Malachi 4:5–6— *"to turn hearts of the fathers to their children"*) took hold. Six of the nine colleges founded between 1740 and 1769—Princeton, Rutgers, Brown, Dartmouth, Pennsylvania, and Columbia—were directly or indirectly affected by revival. George Whitefield influenced the very founding of Dartmouth and Princeton. Princeton's first five presidents were revivalist preachers![5]

But this great revival was followed by a great falling away. I had heard of this before, but when I read about it, I was shocked by what a disastrous fall it truly was! (Apparently, a revival that frightened people with hellfire and brimstone didn't have as much staying power as it would have if it was more balanced with the promise of God's grace.) Just twenty years after the revival, a poll discovered not a single born-again believer among students at Harvard. The much more evangelical Princeton had only two. All but five students at Princeton belonged to the "Filthy Speech Movement," which elevated the most shocking profanity to an artform. Some schools spawned hateful religious prejudice; students held mock communion at Williams College and put on antichristian plays at Dartmouth. A student deist organization stole a Bible from a church in New Jersey and burned it in a public bonfire. To avoid intimidation, some Christian campus groups had to meet in secret.[6]

Off campus, the older generation wasn't faring any better. By 1760, only one in twelve Americans were church members, and in the southern colonies, only one in twenty![7] Americans were the most unchurched people in all of Christendom.[8] Granted, this was partly due to a huge influx of irreligious immigrants, and there was no state church to automatically register every newborn as a member. But the fervency of many First Great Awakening converts had also died away, and vice ran unchecked. Sexual sin was rampant.[9] Gambling and brutal fist fights were favorite pastimes. Fights were so violent that the rule books did not forbid gouging out an opponent's eyes![10] Bank robberies were a daily occurrence. For the first time in American history, women didn't go out at night for fear of being raped.[11] Drunkenness was everywhere, even among church members and pastors![12]

Apparently, during the First Great Awakening, Elijah's call hadn't touched hearts nearly as deeply as it should have. By their example, drunken, brawling fathers were literally cultivating the curse of Malachi 4:5–6, for drunkenness was common even among children![13] Most churches were too dead to address these issues and were losing members. Founding Father Thomas Paine echoed the French philosopher, Voltaire, saying: "Christianity will be forgotten in thirty years."

But a persistent prayer movement set the country ablaze with another revival. Again, Elijah's call began to take hold; concern for the young gripped the hearts of the older generation. During and after the Second Great Awakening (1790–1840), the educational system was reformed and expanded. Churches established forty more colleges, and on many campuses, the flames of revival burned for decades. Evangelist Charles Finney made Oberlin College one of the nation's most important revival centers.[14]

With all this attention focused on youth, it makes sense that young people were the first wave of converts.[15] What those dusty library books (and online histories) taught me is that when young people get the love and mentoring they need, they become world-changers. In Cincinnati, Ohio, Dwight Weld, whom Finney mentored, convinced almost the entire student body of Lane Theological Seminary (including even some southern students) to fight slavery. They opened schools, reading rooms, and libraries for the black community in and around Cincinnati, Ohio. Racist elders at the seminary tried to shut them down, but these kids were not to be denied. They pulled up roots and moved to Oberlin College in Oberlin, Ohio, where, with Finney's fatherly support, Dwight continued his work alongside students of all stripes (Oberlin was one of the first colleges in America to accept black and female students). They converted not only other students, but even slave owners who freed their slaves and became antislavery evangelists! In many other places across the nation, together, young and old advocated universal education, reformed prisons, opposed prostitution, and founded an explosion of new charities.[16]

But again, there was a falling away (although not nearly to the same extent as after the First Great Awakening—probably because of a greater emphasis on grace). And again, revival pulled us back from the brink, in what some have called the "Third Great Awakening" (late 1850's to the early twentieth century). Again, much effort was focused on the young. The YMCA (Young Men's Christian Association) was established to keep young men on the straight and narrow. Young leaders like Dwight Moody were raised up. Youth and their elders worked side by side ministering to traumatized soldiers on both sides of the Civil War.[17] Freedmen's societies provided teachers to set up hundreds of schools in the south for freed slaves and their children.[18]

… But alas, once again, there was a gradual falling away.

As I read, I could see that in some ways, what my friends predicted a future revival will look like did ring true. Yes, it may start off with a bang and spread like wildfire across the land. Yes, in no time, multitudes of new converts might enter the Kingdom. And revival can spark long-lasting cultural changes. But as I sat in my quiet cubicle, contemplating the changes revivals bring, three patterns began to emerge. As I read about other revivals throughout history and around the world, I found that the same was true of them as well.

First, the cultural changes sparked by revivals don't always come quickly. For instance, from the beginning of the First Great Awakening until the Civil War, it took about a hundred and thirty years to stop slavery. It would take another century to abolish the Jim Crow laws that discriminated against blacks. It's easy to make converts; thousands can be gathered into the Kingdom overnight. But the changes started by revivals are carried on by a remnant willing to continue to fight for God's causes at all costs long after the flames of revival have faded.

Second, to one extent or another, there is always a cooling off after every revival, and often a falling away. Revival flames continue burning only in the hearts of the remnant willing to pay the price of rock-solid commitment.

Third, as important as revivals are, there is something God deems far more important. Jesus never commanded His followers to start revivals; He commanded them to make disciples: *"Go therefore and make disciples of all the nations, baptizing them in the name of the Father and the Son and the Holy Spirit, teaching them to follow all that I commanded you"* (Matthew 28:19–20). The extent to which we avoid a falling away is the extent to which the revival is focused on discipleship.

In Scripture, God prepared for every great move of His Spirit in the humblest way—through a family making disciples of its own children. He started the world with a husband-and-wife team—Adam and Eve. He restarted the world with Noah and his wife and their three sons and daughters-in-law. He started Israel with the family of Abraham, Isaac, and Jacob. God could have sent Jesus to us as a grown man, but He chose to have Him raised in a family. Christ started His church with twelve spiritual sons—His apostles.

And we are both His bride and His children. We are a family.

Family is the foundation of everything. The saints have always believed this: in the late 300's AD, St. John Chrysostom said: "The human family constitutes the primary and essential element of human society … Peace in society will be a direct result of peace in the family; order and harmony in the secular, political realm will be a direct result of the order and harmony which arises out of creative guidance and the giving of real responsibility to the children." In the early 1500's, the Catholic saint Angela Merici concurred: "Disorder in society is a result of disorder in the family." In the late 1600's, the Puritan leader, Richard Baxter admonished: "You are not likely to see any general reformation till you procure family reformation."

Before the Second Great Awakening, this was well understood by Christian parents in the Waxhaw region along South Carolina's Catawba River. Elijah's call *"to turn the hearts of fathers to their children"* (Malachi 4:6) burned in the hearts of loving, dutiful fathers who got on their knees alongside their wives and prayed for their prodigals. When revival hit, their newly converted children earnestly reconciled with them.[19] They repented in tears for turning deaf ears to their parents' prayers[20] and then pled in prayer for the souls of their younger brothers and sisters.[21] The curse of Malachi 4:5–6 was lifted! This became the most lasting fruit of the revival.

It also became its driving force. Youth breathed a spark of life into dry religion. They shouted, fainted, wept, and prayed with fervency their parents had never seen. Their parents thought this emotionalism seemed over the top, but they could sense the Holy Spirit in the midst of the mayhem. They preferred this to the mayhem between Christians of their own generation who ridiculed and insulted each other's denominational traditions to the point where some even took up arms. One group actually hired wicked men to harass an itinerant preacher and disrupt his communion service. Someone even released a pack of dogs on members of another church! All this to tout their own brand of stuffy religiosity. Disgusted parents turned away from the hypocrisy and joined in their children's spiritual quest. While they no doubt tempered their rowdiness with the wisdom of age, they defended them from skeptics[22] and helped them pack the churches with people—especially young people—who were desperate for a real relationship with God.

My family knows what the Waxhaw families knew. Family lore has it that an unbroken chain of faith goes back to a time before the

Sandfords landed in the New World. (The first name of a few of our first American ancestors' relatives was "Praying"!) What I know for sure about more recent generations is what I have witnessed in living memory. I think again of the survey that revealed that if a father becomes a Christian, 93% of his family will follow. I see this pattern unfolding in my extended family.

And what an impact they are making on the world! Although Grampa Sandford rebelled against his pastoral calling, at the end of his life, he finally relented. At a reading of his poetry two days before his passing, prompted by the Holy Spirit, he spontaneously preached his first and only sermon. It was on forgiveness and reconciling parents and children! My father carried on the faith with far more resolve. He and Mom answered their call and pastored three churches, founded a worldwide ministry, helped launch several worldwide Christian movements, and wrote many books. Among their descendants and their spouses there are five pastors, eight worship leaders, several church small group leaders, the founder of a parachurch ministry, six published authors of Christian-themed books, a graphic designer for Christian publications, a professor at a Christian University who also transcribes ancient Ethiopian biblical manuscripts, and rising leaders in education, medicine, commerce, and other secular fields. When fathers follow God, their children are blessed into their destinies, and they impact the world. The revival in the family outlasts the revival in the church and keeps the spark alive until the next big revival calls the church back into line with the family.

Not all the Sandfords have excelled at answering Elijah's call to turn our hearts to our children. But most of us have done whatever, in our brokenness, we are capable of, thanking God that He comes through for our children despite our weaknesses. God is gracious. We pray that we'll all continue to persevere in answering Elijah's call.

And we hope to be a part of that last great revival prophesied by so many voices from every corner of Christendom. It has been predicted that through it, multitudes of young people will be gathered into the arms of Jesus. Protestant voices have heralded this for many decades. Catholics have long foreseen an "illumination of conscience" that will call home the prodigals. Nearly a hundred years ago, the Russian Orthodox Saint Seraphim of Viritsa said it best:

There will come a time when corruption and lewdness among the youth will reach the utmost point. There will hardly be any virgin youth left. They will see their lack of punishment and will think that everything is allowable for them to satisfy their desires. God will call them, however, and they will realize that it will not be possible for them to continue such a life. Then in various ways they will be led to God. ... They who formerly were sinners and alcoholics will fill the churches and they will feel great thirst for the spiritual life. ... That time will be beautiful. That today they are sinning greatly, will lead them to a deeper repentance. Just like the candle before it goes out, it shines strongly and throws sparks; with its light, it enlightens the surrounding darkness; thus, it will be the Church's life in the last age. And that time is near.[23]

Believers of every stripe will need that shot in the arm if we are to endure the storm that Jesus prophesied will precede His second coming. Whether this revival will come in our lifetime may depend on what captures our hearts. Will we consider revival our greatest joy? The great nineteenth century Protestant revivalist, Charles Spurgeon, would frown on that. He warned: "If you are professing Christians but cannot say that you have no greater joy than the conversion of your children, you have reason to question whether you ought to have made such a profession at all."

Maureen and I have always prayed and continue to pray that God will turn our hearts toward our children. For that reason, we believe that even if our nation continues its slide into the gutter and a great revival is not forthcoming within our lifetime, we and our children will still have a revival in our own little kitchen.

… But only if we persevere in the practice that is the very source of our joy …

1   Sydney Ahlstrom, *A Religious History of the American People*, 2nd ed. (New Haven, CT and London, UK: Yale University Press, 2004), 287.
2   William Warren Sweet, Peter Smith, *Revivalism in America, Its Origin, Growth, and Decline* (Gloucester, MA: Peter Smith Publishing, 1965), 107.
3   Thomas S. Kidd, *The Great Awakening* (New Haven, CT & London: Yale University Press, 2007), 217.
4   Thomas Kidd, *The Great Awakening: a Brief History with Documents* (Boston, MA and New York, NY: Bedford/St. Martin's, 2007), 19.
5   Sweet and Smith, *Revivalism in America, its Origin, Growth, and Decline*, 147-148.
6   Dr. J. Edwin Orr, "Why Christian Revivals Spark Missionary Advance," Accessed October 28, 2021, http://static1.squarespace.com/static/588ada483a0411af1ab3e7ca/588bbcb95149bfb27161b51c/588bbd305149bfb27161c96e/1485552944169/Why-Revivals-Spark-Missionary-Advance-by-J-Edwin-Orr.pdf?format=original.
7   Sweet and Smith, *Revivalism in America*, 18.
8   William Warren Sweet, *Religion in Colonial America*, (New York, NY, Cooper Square Publishers, Inc., 1965), 334.
9   Sweet and Smith, *Revivalism in America*, 9.
10 Marquies de Castellux, *Travels in North America*, 1780, 1781, 1782, etc. (Dublin, 1787) II, 192–193.
11 Dr. J. Edwin Orr, "Why Christian Revivals Spark."
12 Sweet and Smith, *Revivalism in America*, 107.
13 Sweet and Smith, *Revivalism in America*, 118.
14 Sweet and Smith, *Revivalism in America*, 148-150.
15 Nancy Colt, "Young Women in the Second Great Awakening in New England" *Feminist Studies*, V. 3, No. 1/2 (Autumn, 1975), 16.
16 Sweet and Smith, *Revivalism in America*, 157-159.
17 Sweet and Smith, *Revivalism in America*, 160-161.
18 Richard Gause Boone, *Education in the United States: Its History from the Earliest Settlements* (Freeport, NY: Books for Libraries Press, 1889, 1971), 351.
19 Peter N. Moore, "Family Dynamics and the Great Revival; Religious Conversion in the South Carolina Piedmont," *The Journal of Southern History*, Vol. 70, No. 1 (February, 2004), 38, JSTOR, https://www.jstor.org/stable/27648311.
20 Peter N. Moore, "Family Dynamics and the Great Revival," 60.
21 Peter N. Moore, "Family Dynamics and the Great Revival," 59.
22 Peter N. Moore, "Family Dynamics and the Great Revival," 60.
23 St. Seraphim of Viritsa, *Life, Miracles, and Prophecies of Saint Seraphim of Viritsa: The New Saint of Orthodox Russian Church 1866–1949* (Thessaloniki, Greece: Orthodox Kypseli Publications, 2005), 44–45.

CHAPTER 20

Repentance—the Window on Joy

IT'S HARD TO MAKE REPENTANCE your lifestyle if your picture of it evokes only sorrow. I could explain, but as they say, a picture is worth a thousand words. I recently viewed an insightful painting by Ben McPherson titled *Repentance*. He expertly portrays how so many people view repentance. In the picture, behind a stubborn little boy looms an angry old nun, her fiery eyes fixed fiercely on her task, her lips pursed with determination. With both hands, she carefully centers a glowing yellow halo directly above the boy's head. The halo illuminates her wizened face from below like a hollow-eyed demonic apparition emerging from the shadows. The boy puffs out his cheeks as if holding his breath. With concealed defiance, he purses his lips more tightly than she purses hers. He strains to stand up tall and fill a man's baggy shirt three sizes too large for him. His body language declares that though he wears the halo, in his heart he refuses to submit. But as I viewed the painting, I could tell that under all that billowing fabric, he feels small and weak.

I imagined how alone this little boy must feel. For him, repentance evokes emotions too scary to look at. Overwhelming shame about whatever naughty thing he has done. Fierce anger at the one who is rubbing his nose in it. He'll need someone to lead him to a God whose tender grace will take the edge off that pain. He doesn't dare allow it to leak out in the presence of the domineering matron towering above him. Will he share it with his parents? Or are they off the edge of the canvas, turning a blind eye or even looking upon this scene with approval? If so, the boy may choose to hide his feelings even from himself and go numb.

If repentance is the medicine for a sin-sick heart, to this boy the cure seems worse than the illness. But that's only because he has never tasted the real medicine. Since the "repentance" thrust upon him is divorced from comfort, he may close his heart to the heavenly Comforter. When he is older, where will he then find comfort? Shots of meth? Backseat liaisons? If he invites Jesus into his heart but the numbness lingers, what then will become his drug of choice? The thrill of the quest for supernatural experiences and personal prophecies? Even sacred comforts become addictions when they replace the Comforter Himself.

That can easily happen when you see repentance as nothing more than turning away from sin. It truly is that, but so much more. A Hebrew Old Testament word for "repentance," *nacham*, means "sorrow." But when sorrow about guilt is all there is, you become the little boy in the painting, and an addiction can seem like the only relief. Another Hebrew word for "repentance," *shub*, and the New Testament Greek word, *metanoia*, mean "to turn." Repentance isn't just turning away from the sins about which we feel sorrowful. It is turning toward the source of joy Who comforts the sorrow that sins have brought upon the sinner.

Forty years ago, an old friend, Katherine, showed me what this looks like firsthand. "I never understood 1 Timothy 1:15," she said. "*'Christ Jesus came into the world to save sinners—of whom I **am** the*

worst' [NIV]. Not **was** the worst! St. Paul was old by then; He'd been through a lifetime of repentance. So how could he call himself 'the worst of sinners' so nonchalantly? If he still was 'the worst of sinners,' didn't he feel ashamed about that? I had always felt like I was the worst of sinners, and I drowned in shame! I grew up being blamed by my family for things I didn't even do. My classmates bullied me, and two of my teachers would laugh right along with them despite my being an 'A' student who never got into trouble. My mom would put her arm around my brother's shoulder and tousle his hair playfully, but she would never hug or touch me or even let herself be alone with me."

Katherine lowered her voice slightly, and her tone became more grave. "It wasn't until I was an adult that I realized that, deep in Mom's heart, she knew Dad was molesting me. She wouldn't be alone with me for fear I might say something about it and she'd have to confront him, knowing he would do one of two things—throw her out with us kids, or throw her out and keep the four of us. That's probably why I buried the memory and never told Mom; I didn't want that to happen. When I grew up, I married an abusive alcoholic who divorced me. My older daughter got pregnant out of wedlock. My younger daughter became so rebellious I was forced to put her in a foster home. My husband hadn't fixed the car—as usual—so I had to carry her belongings on foot twelve blocks to the health and welfare office where I left her with a foster couple. I cried so hard all the way home I couldn't see where I was going!"

Even as Katherine described the shame and sorrow, her eyes still radiated joy.

"When I discovered inner healing, I found hope; now I could confess all my roots of bitterness. At first, it felt wonderful! I thought, 'At last I can clean up this mess inside me!' I could become the good child I'd always wanted to be. But the Lord kept showing me more and more roots of bitterness until I felt like a bottomless pit of bitterness. I started feeling hopeless again, like I was the worst of sinners. But every time I turned to God and repented for another layer of bitterness, I felt His warmth, like He was saying, 'Don't you know I love you no matter what you've done?' It took a hundred repentances before something finally clicked and I got it. A deep, infinite love flowed over me that I never knew existed. Now, when God shows me something more to repent of, I say, 'Thank You Lord for not letting me get away with that one!' And I say it joyfully! I never thought repentance could make me feel so loved! I really do understand why Paul could feel okay calling himself 'the worst of sinners.'"

In the decades since that conversation, every time I have seen Katherine, the joy in her eyes has shone brighter than before. Recently, having been apart for a long while, I gave her a call. The intervening season had not been kind to her. She had just gotten out of the hospital and was slowly recovering from a host of ailments, including colitis, low blood pressure, and a rare bacterial infection. For the past two years she had lived much of her days in the bathroom. She couldn't eat foods she loved. She was too weak to drive. She was unable to visit beloved old friends in Ireland where she had owned a bed-and-breakfast for twenty years. But I heard no resentment in her voice. That resilient joy resounded more clearly than ever, and I wanted to know more about it.

"Tell me what you've learned in the forty years since we had that conversation about 1 Timothy."

"I've learned that every time I repent, there's no condemnation; I don't have to do everything perfectly to be acceptable. I've learned that every grief about the way I've been treated draws me toward a gracious, loving God. And that digs a deeper cavern to contain the joy that Jesus loves me no matter how bitter I've been toward people who've hurt me."

Katherine had learned what the saints have always known about repentance. In the early 600's AD, St. John Climacus said, "To repent is to look, not downward at my own shortcomings, but upward at God's love; not backward with self-reproach, but forward with trustfulness. It is to see, not what I have failed to be, but what by the grace of Christ I might yet become."

Katherine's life-compass had turned unswervingly upward and forward. Excitedly, she continued: "There's no unforgiveness left in my heart toward anyone who hurt me, only joy."

As a counselor, I had learned to spot people in denial. There was no denial here. Katherine had fully forgiven; her joy was real. "For many years now, I've realized I just love people. It's not an effort; it's just me being who God created me to be. And people love me as well. In the hospital, one of my nurses told another nurse, 'When the buzzer goes off, she's the only one I'd literally run down the hall for!' And my daughters are wonderful to me now! With all my ailments, they never see me as a burden. They take better care of me than I ever took care of them. When God enabled me to forgive, that's what opened my heart to accept love from family and friends and even strangers and to become more and more a reflection of Him, which is really the purpose of each one of us here on earth."

Long ago, Katherine had discarded the self-imposed halo; she no longer had need of its paltry light. She was now wearing a real one. Even on the phone, I could picture her luminous eyes—those gateways to heaven in elderly souls who have discovered through hardships and having to turn to God in desperation again and again, that repentance is the window through which shines the light of joy.

… And that it is the doorway to revival.

There is a world of young people out there (and old ones too), standing up straight, pursing their lips, trying their best to be good girls and boys. They accept the sorrow of repentance as a morose necessity, a religious duty that earns the halo. Too many of them are looking for joy in the things of God instead of the person of God because they see Him as the old nun in the painting. And they wonder why joy is so elusive.

It is time to take our light out from under the bushel, place it in the window, draw our curtains wide, and watch as this beacon leads them to our door.

CHAPTER 21

Revival Starts in the Kitchen, Not in the Auditorium

WHEN THE CURTAINS ARE DRAWN wide on a repentant soul, the world sees a God big enough to hold seemingly contradictory truths. Jesus said, *"Whoever does not receive the Kingdom of God like a little child will not enter it at all"* (Mark 10:15), but St. Paul said, *"When I became a man, I did away with childish things"* (1 Corinthians 13:11). The older Katherine gets, the more of a child she becomes, while our three children blossom into the glory of adulthood.

Until forgiveness and repentance become a lifestyle, one can be neither mature nor childlike, only childish. I envision Baal perched on his distant throne, looking more and more like a toddler dangling his little legs off the edge of his highchair. As our family has continued to offer each other repentance and forgiveness, in our eyes, he has shrunk down to what he truly is: a "pathetic little nothing."

Maureen and I don't see our children lusting after Baal's enticements. We don't even see them lusting after the enticements of God's miracles. We see them simply seeking after God. For that reason, we have no doubt that in their lifetime they will see more than their share of His miracles ... and a revival around their own kitchen tables.

When our children were small, I often forgot all the miracles God had done for our family. In difficult times, I pleaded, "Why aren't you there for us?" But in my saner moments, I remembered. So, to keep myself from forgetting again, I began to type each of them into a computer file as they occurred. To prove that these were not coincidences, I recorded only the ones that couldn't easily be explained away as such. There were the many times when the Holy Spirit warned Maureen and me to pray for protection and we and our children were spared from injuries, death, and even kidnappings. There were the copious times He provided in the most unexpected ways the exact amount needed to pay a bill, fund an adventure, or help a friend in need. And there were the times when God prompted us to pray, and He answered by changing the world beyond our front door in very specific and sometimes dramatic ways. But it wasn't until I typed quite a few of them that it really sank in that God is there for me and that He turns to me with undeserved grace far more often than I even think to turn back to Him in repentance. And it wasn't until I had typed quite a few more that, like Katherine, I finally felt the joy of that grace.

For me, the bigger miracles were the most exciting. But I suspect that the miracles that most affected our children were the little favors God did just for them. Like the time when our new kitten had wandered away. Maureen called me at work and, with a frantic edge in her voice, pled, "Mark, please pray that I can find Romeo! I can just imagine how it'll affect the kids if we don't find him!" A few minutes later, I called back to tell her I sensed he was near an intersection three blocks north of our house. Maureen didn't answer; she was already out searching. So, I prayed that God would lead her to Romeo. She felt the Holy Spirit's prompting to walk north and knock on doors until at last, she reached a house near that very intersection. A woman came to the door, and beside her stood her little daughter, holding Romeo (she had thought she had rescued a stray). We were scheduled for a ministry trip to Pennsylvania two days later; now the kids were no longer afraid of our leaving. They knew that God would watch out for them while we were gone.

Sixteen years later, we were wondering what to get for Míchal's birthday. Another kitten? (Romeo was no longer with us.) We prayed that if God wanted a kitten for her, He would bring one to us. The next morning after church, someone found a box of kittens abandoned behind the building. A little yellow tabby whom Míchal named "Tiggy" became her companion through one of the loneliest seasons of her life. The miracles that won her heart to God were not the "impressive" ones that impacted the vast world beyond our door. They were the ones that proved He cared about what was important to her. God cared about kittens.

It was always the little things that made the difference. Like the time when Maureen felt prompted to take Jasha and his friend Ryan to Game Haven in Coeur d'Alene where kids gathered for tabletop fun.

"We've already planned to take Jasha there next week," I protested. "There are other things we need to do right now. Why not wait?"

"I just know it's urgent," Maureen answered. "I sense the Holy Spirit is saying I have to take him there this week before something bad happens."

I trusted Maureen's discernment, and she did as God had prompted. A few days later, Game Haven burned to the ground. But Jasha hadn't missed his last chance to go there. Nor had he missed the message his sensitive heart needed to hear—that even when the world around him is on fire and sirens are blaring for attention, God is focused on what's important to Jasha.

If repentance is turning toward God, children learn it in all the little moments when God turns toward them simply because He loves them, not just when there's a sin to confess. He does that especially through parents. Our children learned it when Maureen took them shopping at second-hand stores and let them pick out a low-budget treasure to take home. They learned it when she made not only birthday cakes, but pink Valentine's Day cakes and green St. Patrick's Day cakes and even red, white, and blue Fourth of July cakes. They learned it when they all piled into a sleeping bag with me and we slid together, giggling down the stairs, night after night until the seams began to rip.

When our children needed to turn their hearts toward us to confess a wrongdoing, memories of us turning our hearts toward them were the spoonful of sugar that made the medicine go down. They had come to expect that the tenderness didn't cease when it was time for us to hear their confessions.

"I'm bad," said Jonah after I disciplined him for typical four-year-old naughtiness. I sat him next to me on our bed and wrapped my arm around him.

"You are not bad, Jonah. You're a good boy. Good people sometimes do bad things, but it doesn't make them bad people."

Jonah kept hanging his head in shame and shrank from my embrace.

"When you do something bad, that's not who you are. Even when you do bad things, I'm still proud of who you are. Nothing you do will ever change the way I see you."

Jonah raised his chin slightly and leaned into my side. Maureen came in and sat down on the other side of Jonah. She put her arm around him and told him how proud of him she was and how much we loved him no matter what.

"I'm sorry for what I did," said Jonah. Those words were easier to say now; there was no shame in them anymore.

We told him he was forgiven, hugged him, and prayed aloud, "Thank you, Jesus, for Jonah, for what a good boy he is." We kissed his cheeks from both sides, and he ran off to play, feeling forgiven and knowing in his heart that repentance truly is the window to joy.

… And knowing it is also the exercise that builds strength to do hard things.

Many years later, I witnessed Jonah being treated callously by a Christian leader, and I failed to stand up for him. In the shock of the moment, I froze. My mind was present, but my heart was not. It was stranded on a Kansas farm where no one stood up to the rapists. It was alone in an eighth grade P.E. class where no one stood up to the bullies. All my life, I had been incapable of returning my heart to the present where I could invest it in defending myself or anyone else.

Three years later, inner healing had caused more of my emotional pain killer to wear off, and I had begun to feel—really feel—what it was like when no one stood up for me. And now I could feel what Jonah felt when I didn't stand up for him. I called him on the phone and told him I was beginning to feel how horribly dishonored he must have felt after all the excellent work he had done. "Will you forgive me for not standing up for you?" I asked. Not that I hadn't asked his forgiveness for this before. But now I could say it with real empathy.

Jonah forgave. I knew that he would, because Baal's plan for a life of spiritual ease had found no place in his heart. He had learned to do hard things, like forgiving. He could forgive me because he had learned that sometimes fathers do bad things, but that doesn't mean they are bad fathers. His forgiveness was one of the many little miracles that have told me that God is thinking of me, too.

Why does God send Elijah to turn the hearts of fathers to their children and the hearts of children to their fathers? Because the family is where we learn how to repent and forgive. That is the miracle that will keep the curse of Malachi 4:5–6 from bringing destruction on our land.

If repentance leads to revival, then the family leads to revival. Revival must start in the kitchen, not in the auditorium. It must start with the issues of everyday life.

CHAPTER 22

Elijah is Waiting

FOR A SEASON, EVERY NIGHT at bedtime, Dad read a story to his children that drove home the message of where revival really begins. An ancient and mysterious gold ring, long-lost, had been rediscovered. The powers of darkness could sense the presence of the ring and were on the hunt for it, for they believed that whoever had charge of it could rule the world! *The Lord of The Rings* was the tale of a fellowship of two humans, an elf, a dwarf, a wizard, and four hobbits who set out on a journey to save the ring from falling into evil hands. The ring itself wanted to be found—by the forces of evil. If that wasn't possible, it would try to seduce the very persons commissioned to destroy it. Anyone who slipped the ring on his finger would be duped into thinking he had acquired its power and was hidden from all attackers, but the ring would only make him visible and vulnerable to the powers of darkness.

Who was up to the task of bearing such a ponderous burden to the heart of Mt. Doom and dropping it into the lava to destroy it? Not a human, an elf, or a dwarf. Not even the wise old wizard, Gandalf. One of the little people was chosen, for hobbits understood better than anyone what it was that needed saving—the simple joys of the shire: first and second breakfast, tea and crumpets, afternoon walks on the heather, and lively banter and raucous laughter across a table with friends and family. Hobbits knew how to cherish the little everyday miracles of life. Thus, only a hobbit like Frodo, aided by his loyal friend, Sam, could resist the seduction of the more "impressive" supernatural powers the ring had to offer.

I think it was not just the brilliant writing or clever storyline that held us spellbound. It was that the book confirmed something we were already learning at home—that it is not the swords of humans, the cunning of elves, the strength of dwarves, or the power and wisdom of wizards that can vanquish the evil hordes that threaten to engulf the masses. In our world, He who would vanquish them became one of the little people. He was born in the humblest of circumstances and was laid in a farm animal's manger. He learned the lessons of love and life in his mother's lap and his father's carpenter's shop. As an adult, when He taught others what he had learned, He expressed it through the imagery of the little people, like a farmer who planted his field or a shepherd who found his lost sheep. Everyone expected him to set up a magnificent throne on Zion from which He would rule the entire earth with an iron scepter. To fulfill such a cause, they expected much loftier training. But His humble training was far better preparation for a cause far more infinite—to save the little people from eternal death by His own death, and by His resurrection, to give them eternal life. His heavenly Father knew that family life was the best preparation for this because He knew something they didn't know ...

... that it is milk and cookies that will change the world.

Every night we would beg, "Please, Dad, read us one more chapter!" Often, he would, and then we would beg for another. But he would fold the book and say, "Time for little hobbits to be off to bed!" Sometimes Mom would sing us to sleep as she tucked us in, her operatic voice lowered to a feathery whisper, and our day would end on a note of wonder.

As I savor that memory, the little boy in the painting, *Repentance,* comes to mind, and I feel sorry that he hasn't discovered that same wonder in the heart of God. "But perhaps he will," I think hopefully, "if only a spiritual mother or father will show him the joy that awaits him on the other side of true repentance."

In my mind's eye, another painting comes into view, looking much like Da Vinci's *Last Supper.* Jesus is seated at the center of the table with his twelve disciples gathered around him. He is serving them bread and wine—the spiritual meal of the ages. I back up for a broader perspective, and on the periphery, Mom and Dad, my brothers and sisters, Maureen and the kids, and Maureen's family come into view. I back up farther, and the scene expands to include longsuffering Gary. He has returned from his talk with Jeremy. He has shown him his nail scars, and Jeremy has followed him back to the banquet. I see Thomas, looking stronger than ever with Esther at his side. I see Mark whom I met on the plane. There's humble Tobias and his earnest descendant and namesake, Tobias. Jamison, Josiah, Layne, and Shawna sit still and stalwart, like rocks braced against the storm. Ben and Mike are sharing a father-son embrace. Rose Marie the "angel lady," dear old Mary Mott, and joyful Katherine are once again serving at this table of life. I look to each horizon and see that the table goes on forever. I perceive that part of it once went through Mary's kitchen, and I realize more than ever what a banquet she really served.

In the midst of them all, I see Elijah nodding approvingly because he knows this is a painting that truly portrays the fruit of repentance that leads to *theosis*—that deepest intimacy with the Father that transforms us with ever-increasing glory into His likeness. Elijah views in this masterpiece a fellowship of children who have turned back to Father God countless times until they have learned—not only in their minds but in their hearts—that the bread Jesus serves and the wine He pours is a covenant He'll never break. They have learned that this promise stands no matter how many times they fail to keep their covenant with Him or with their children, as long as they keep turning back to Him whenever they fall. Having been forgiven seventy times seven, the eyes of their hearts have been opened to see the lovingkindness and forbearance that was always there for them. That is what keeps them coming back for more. It's what enables them to repent without ceasing until their hearts are transformed. God's love has made repentance a joy, and in their hearts, revival has already begun.

Out of the low-pitched rumble of table-talk, I hear someone remark, "Who would have thought that something as humble as milk and cookies could have led us to a banquet such as this?"

I see Elijah rise from his chair. He loads up a heaping silver tray with cookies, balances a pitcher beside them, and carries it all to the door. He opens it wide and holds forth the tray as he calls out to everyone: "Do you want to prevent the curse from coming upon your land? Do you really want to change the world? Where, then, will you begin?"

… And he waits for an answer.

BIBLIOGRAPHY

Ahltstrom, Sydney. *A Religious History of the American People*, 2nd ed. New Haven, CT and London, UK: Yale University Press, 2004.

American Bible Society. "Canaanite Gods and Goddesses." Accessed February 23, 2021. bibleresources.american.org/resoursce/Canaanite-gods-and-goddesses.

Bailey, Kenneth. *Jesus Through Middle Eastern Eyes*. Downers Grove, IL: Intervarsity Press, 2008.

Bailey, Kenneth. "The Cross and the Prodigal." Lecture, Denver Theological Seminary, Englewood, CO, April, 1981.

Barna. "Prodigal Pastors' Kids: Fact or Fiction?" (November 11, 2013). Accessed September 4, 2020. https://www.barna.com/research/prodigal-pastor-kids-fact-or-fiction/.

Bible Reading Archaeology. "Did the Canaanites Really Sacrifice Their Children?". May 13, 2018. Accessed February 12. 2021, https://biblereadingarcheology.com/2016/05/13/did-the-canaanites-sacrifice-their-children/.

Boone, Richard Gause. *Education in the United States: Its History from the Earliest Settlements*. Freeport, NY: Books for Libraries Press, 1889, 1971.

Bowen, Barbara M. *Strange Scriptures that Perplex the Western Mind*. Grand Rapids, MI: Wm B. Eerdmans Publishing Company, 1944.

Brooks, David. *The Atlantic.* "The Nuclear Family Was a Mistake" (March 2020). Accessed April 5, 2021. theatlantic.com/magazine/archive/2020/03/the-nuclear-family-was-a-mistake/605536/.

Brown, Christopher A. *The Father Factor.* "What's the Status of Father Absence Ahead of the Twenty Twenty Census?". Accessed September 3, 2020. https://www.fatherhood.org/fatherhood/father-absence-ahead-of-the-2020-census.

Catholic Online. "St. John of the Cross." Accessed Feb 2, 2021. https://www.catholic.org/saints/saint.php?saint_id=65.

Census Bureau. "More Children Live with Just Their Fathers than a Decade Ago" (November 16, 2017). Accessed August 28, 2020. https://www.census.gov/newsroom/press-releases/2017/living-arrangements.html.

Colt, Nancy. "Young Women in the Second Great Awakening in New England." *Feminist Studies,* V. 3, No. 1/2 (Autumn, 1975): 16.

Cohn, D'Vera. *PRB.* "Do Parents Spend Enough Time With Their children?". January 17, 2007. Accessed November 1, 2021. https://www.prb.org/resources/do-parents-spend-enough-time-with-their-children/.

Cunningham, Lawrence. *America the Jesuit Review.* "Who was St. John of the Cross?". January 30, 2006. Accessed Feb. 2, 2021, https://www.americamagazine.org/faith/2006/01/30/who-was-st-john-cross.

Encyclopedia.com. Fertility and Vegetation Cults (In the Bible)." Accessed February 2021. https://www.encyclopedia.com/religion/encyclopedias-almanacs-transcripts-and-maps/fertility-and-vegetation-cults-bible.

Fathers.com. "More Data on the Extent of Fatherlessness." Accessed August 31, 2020.

 https://fathers.com/statistics-and-research/the-extent-of- fatherlessness/

The Fatherless Generation. "Statistics." Accessed August 6, 2020. https://thefatherlessgeneration.wordpress. com/statistics/.

Freeman, James M. *Manners and Customs of the Bible.* Plainfield, NJ: Logos International, 1972.

The Heritage Foundation. "The Importance of Dads in an Increasingly Fatherless America." Accessed August 6. 2020, https://www.heritage.org/marriage-and-family/commentary/the importance-dads-increasingly-fatherless-america.

ICS Publications, Institute of Carmelite Studies. "St. John of the Cross—Conflicts of Jurisdiction." Accessed Feb 3, 2021. https://www.icspublications.org/pages/saint-john-of-the-cross-conflicts-of-jurisdiction.

Jeremias, Joachim. *Jerusalem in the Time of Jesus.* Philadelphia, PA: Fortress Press, 1969.

Kidd, Thomas S. *The Great Awakening* (New Haven, CT & London: Yale University Press, 2007).

Kidd, Thomas. *The Great Awakening: a Brief History with Documents.* Boston, MA and New York, NY: Bedford/St. Martin's, 2007.

Lewis, C.S. *The Great Divorce.* New York, NY: Collier Books, MacMillan Publishing Co., 1946.

Livingston, Gretchen and Kim Parker. *Pew Research Center, Social and Demographic Trends.* "A Tale of Two Fathers, More are Active, But More Are Absent." Accessed September 4, 2020. https://www.pewsocialtrends.org/2011/06/15/a-tale-of-two-fathers/.

Marquies de Castellux. *Travels in North America* 1780,1781, 1782, etc. Dublin, 1787 II.

Merrill, Eugene H. *Kingdom of Priests.* Grand Rapids, MI: Baker Publishing Group, 2008.

Modern Mom. "Child Behavior Problems With an Absent Mother." Accessed August 28, 2020. https://www.modernmom.com/79653770-3b45-11e3-8407-bc764e04a41e.html.

Moore, Peter N. "Family Dynamics and the Great Revival; Religious Conversion in the South Carolina Piedmont." *The Journal of Southern History,* V. 70, No. 1. JSTOR (February, 2004): 38. https://www.jstor.org/stable/27648311.

Nami (National Alliance on Mental Health Issues). "Mental Health by the Numbers." Accessed September 1, 2020. https://www.nami.org/mhstats.

New World Encyclopedia. "Baal." Accessed Feb 6, 2021. newworldencyclopedia.org/entry/baal.

Dr. J. Edwin Orr, "Why Christian Revivals Spark Missionary Advance," Accessed October 28, 2021, http://static1.squarespace.com/static/588ada483a0411af1ab3e7ca/588bbcb95149bfb27161b51c/588bbd305149bfb27161c96e/1485552944169/Why-Revivals-Spark-Missionary-Advance-by-J-Edwin-Orr.pdf?format=original.

Ortiz-Ospina, Esteban. *Our World in Data.* "Are Parents Spending Less Time With Their Kids?", December 14, 2020. Accessed October 30, 2021. https://ourworldindata.org/parents-time-with-kids.

Schulte, Brigid. *The Washington Post.* "Making Time for Kids? Study Says Quality Trumps Quality." March 28, 2015. Accessed November 1, 2021. https://www.washingtonpost.com/local/making-time-for-kids-study-says-quality-trumps-quantity/2015/03/28/10813192-d378-11e4-8fce-3941fc548f1c_story.html.

Science Daily. "Mental health issues increased significantly in young adults over last decade" (March 15, 2019). Accessed September 1, 2020. https://www.sciencedaily.com/releases/2019/03/190315110908.htm.

St. Athanasius. *On the Incarnation.*

St. John of the Cross, E. Allison Peers, translator. *Dark Night of the Soul.* Mineola, NY: Dover Publications Inc., 2003.

St. Seraphim of Viritsa. *Life, Miracles, and Prophecies of Saint Seraphim of Viritsa: The New Saint of Orthodox Russian Church 1866-1949.* Thessaloniki, Greece: Orthodox Kypseli Publications, 2005.

Sweet, William Warren. *Religion in Colonial America.* New York, NY, Cooper Square Publishers, Inc., 1965.

Sweet, William Warren, and Peter Smith. *Revivalism in America, Its Origin, Growth, and Decline.* Gloucester, MA:, Peter Smith Publishing, 1965.

United States Census Bureau. "The Majority of Children Live With Two parents, Census Bureau Reports." November 17, 2016. Accessed August 31, 2020. https://www.census.gov/newsroom/press-releases/2016/cb16192.html.

Walton, John H., Victor H. Matthews and Mark W. Chavalas. *The IVP Bible Background Commentary, Old Testament.* Downers Grove, IL: Intervarsity Press, 2000).

Wight, Fred. *Manners and Customs of Bible Lands.* Chicago, IL: Moody Press 1953.

Wood, Steve. *Dads.org.* "Why the New Evangelization Needs a Focus on Fathers" (February 22, 2016). Accessed September 4, 2020. https://dads.org/fatherhood/why-the-new-evangelization-needs-a-focus-on-fathers/.

You Are Mom. "How an Absent Mother Affects Children." Accessed August 28, 2020. https://youaremom.com/children/absent-mother-affects-children/.

MINISTRIES

———• **Mark Sandford** •———

Mark Sandford is cofounder, with his wife Maureen, of Elijah Rain Ministries. He earned a bachelor of Fine Arts from Boise State University and a Master of Divinity in Counseling from Denver Theological Seminary. Building on the foundation laid by his parents, John and Paula Sandford, he teaches and writes on inner healing, deliverance, the prophetic, and other subjects and heals hearts through prayer counseling. He shares life and love with his partner in ministry, Maureen, and his three children, Míchal, Jonah, and Jasha.

elijahrainministries.org

CPSIA information can be obtained
at www.ICGtesting.com
Printed in the USA
LVHW111637110522
718513LV00006B/98